*For Marilyn and Ed
From an old friend.
Denis Bayton Knight*

Joyride
FOR SALE

Joyride FOR SALE

Laughing and Living in
Short Little Pieces

Dennis Payton Knight

Copyright © 2014 Dennis Payton Knight.

All rights reserved. No part of this book may be used or reproduced by any means, graphic, electronic, or mechanical, including photocopying, recording, taping or by any information storage retrieval system without the written permission of the publisher except in the case of brief quotations embodied in critical articles and reviews.

Archway Publishing books may be ordered through booksellers or by contacting:

Archway Publishing
1663 Liberty Drive
Bloomington, IN 47403
www.archwaypublishing.com
1-(888)-242-5904

Because of the dynamic nature of the Internet, any web addresses or links contained in this book may have changed since publication and may no longer be valid. The views expressed in this work are solely those of the author and do not necessarily reflect the views of the publisher, and the publisher hereby disclaims any responsibility for them.

Any people depicted in stock imagery provided by Thinkstock are models, and such images are being used for illustrative purposes only. Certain stock imagery © Thinkstock.

ISBN: 978-1-4808-0712-9 (sc)
ISBN: 978-1-4808-0714-3 (hc)
ISBN: 978-1-4808-0713-6 (e)

Library of Congress Control Number: 2014940192

Printed in the United States of America.

Archway Publishing rev. date: 5/14/2014

For Thomas and Alyssa

Remembering Robert

Contents

Preface _____ xi
Acknowledgments _____ xiii
Joyride for Sale _____ 1
My Career as a Male Belly Dancer _____ 3
Football, Autumn Leaves, and Cinders _____ 5
How to Iron a Shirt: A Bachelor's Primer _____ 7
My Bucket List _____ 9
The Day the House Blew Up _____ 11
My Dad, a Character _____ 13
Are We There Yet? _____ 15
The Personality Transplant _____ 17
A Morning at the Museum _____ 19
Out Standing in My Field _____ 21
Mr. Manners on Elevator Etiquette _____ 23
The Kiddy Show _____ 25
The Day the Music Slowed: A Love Affair _____ 27
There Ought to Be a Law _____ 29
Summer Vacation _____ 31
Home Economics 101 for Boys _____ 33
Searching for the Meaning of Life _____ 35
I'm an Old Cowhand _____ 37
Let 'er Blow _____ 39
My Favorite Animal Family _____ 41
Dad and the Buick Woody _____ 43
Just Kidding _____ 45
My Grandmother's Diary _____ 47

Strawberries	49
Food for Thought	51
The International Happiness of Pancakes	53
The Nearsighted Sharpshooter	55
Parade of Tubas, Tutus, Taiko, and Towing	57
The Back of My Book	59
Music Made in America	61
Presidential 'Dos	63
Uncle Tom	65
The Solstices—Marking the Extremes	67
The International Happiness of Ice Cream	69
Under the Rainbow	71
Questions in the Carnage	73
The Silver Dollar Tossel	75
Dad's Canary	77
Put That in Your Pipe	79
The Nattering Gnat	81
A Letter to My Tattoo Artist	83
It Started at the Tower of Babel	85
Storytellers, Once Upon a Time	87
My Time in the Arena	89
Old Dogs, New Tricks	91
The Twelve Days of Christmas, Plus One	93
Money and Might	97
The Winter Solstice or Happy New Year	99
The Last Thing on Her List	101
Atmosphere at the Columbine Steakhouse	103
My Advanced Youth, the Early Stages	105
A Monkey Wrench in the Works	107

The Desperate Deed	109
Rolling in Rallods	111
Yes, Dear	113
♪ My Father's Big Hands	115
A One-Man Band Called Luigi	117
Space	119
Murder by Mary McGuire	121
What I Missed in Kindergarten	123
The Little White Church in Virginia Dale	125
Uncle Joyce Kilgore	127
Worry and Wonder	129
Blue	131
Labor Day Is for the Bees	133
Still Growing Up	135
An Open Letter to Newton Minow	137
Trust Me	139
A Gobbled History of the Turkey	141
A Fly in the Oval Office	143
A Grumpy Old Imaginer	145
Christmas Magic and How I Survived It	147
The Life and Times of Pixie Homaly Domaly	149
Buckets and Buckets	151
A Mousekin Christmas	153
White Lies and Puffery	155
Stars and Stripes and Sousa Forever	157
An Introduction to Chindogu	159
Making It Home	161
Live to Learn	163

Preface

My highest goal for this book is that you will laugh aloud at something I have written. I consider myself in the genre of humorists, but if you agree, it will not be simply because I gave you a giggle or a guffaw, but because I helped you to be in a state of good humor.

If I want to provide you with something to laugh at, a punch line or silly non sequitur will usually do it. If my piece needs *someone* to laugh at, then I take the cue from my personal literary idol, James Thurber: "The wit makes fun of other persons; the satirist makes fun of the world; the humorist makes fun of himself."

Of the short little pieces that constitute this volume, some are from real life, others are fictional flights of absurdity, and a few are but simple observations of the world, wry ones, if I am lucky. Some I believe are funny and some are not, but they all come from an optimistic and perhaps quirky perspective that carries me through life.

Please join me on this joyride. If we have some laughs and good conversation along the way, the book will have met all my expectations, and I will count myself a millionaire *Rolling in Rallods*.

ACKNOWLEDGMENTS

Most of the short little pieces that constitute this book I created as a member of the Windsor Gardens Writers Group in Denver. It is an inspiring forum of talented and inventive people, and I owe them my thanks.

Thank you to family and friends who have encouraged me to assemble this collection.

If I am a lifelong learner, I owe it to generations of role models and mentors, some my elders, others my contemporaries, and often those who are younger, including my sons and their cousins.

Thank you to the folks at Archway Publishing who have seen to it that I did it right.

Joyride for Sale

I hope you are in a mood to buy, because today I am selling. I do not have brushes, a time-share, or a bridge, just the notion that joy is the shiny vehicle that carries us through life.

Now, before I make my pitch, let me begin with a disclaimer. I have had failures and disappointments, small and large. I have lost parents, a brother, and a marriage, and I have outlived a son. I am ultimately shaped not only by whom I have known and what I have gained but by what and whom I have lost. If I am not the better for it, at least I have a stronger appreciation for life and the importance of finding joy in the journey. I know you, too, have had your ups and downs, and I'm probably preaching to the choir.

This week, I was clicking through the channels and paused to watch a five-second news teaser of a young boy, maybe three, with a brand-new cochlear implant, hearing his father's voice for the first time. He rose from his seat, his eyes searched for the source of the vibration, and, making the connection, joy and amazement filled him. I didn't need to wait for the story because his beaming face already told it. It was a moment his family and doctors will not forget, and it gave me a smile and a drop in the ocean of joy that floats my boat.

"Field and forest, vale and mountain, blooming meadow, flashing sea, chanting bird and flowing fountain, call us to rejoice in Thee." This stanza is from a hymn set to the music of Beethoven's "Ode to Joy," and it says in a few words everything I am trying to sell you today.

There is joy in the sunrise of a new day, and even if it turns into one of sorrow and loss, it always ends with the promise of a new tomorrow. A soldier on the battlefield or a child in a bomb shelter, isolated from all we find wonderful, will find joy in these things, if nothing else.

Joy is a Viennese waltz, Glenn Miller's "A String of Pearls," a Beatles composition, or Johnny Cash on the "Orange Blossom Special." Today, I heard the tight harmony of the Manhattan Transfer grooving on a Sunday afternoon, and it made my day.

There is joy in that harbinger of spring, the first dandelion, joy in knowing it's not mine to battle, and a reminder to me of the joy of living where I do. There is joy in good news. My friend and neighbor, who is my Saturday shopping companion, called to tell me she went swimming this morning. Her excitement was contagious and another drop in my own ocean of joy. She is going again tomorrow.

I remember the joys of childhood and the sizzling aroma of bacon wafting from the kitchen to charm my brothers and me from our bunks like snakes from a basket. I remember summer afternoons perched on a cottonwood branch, quite satisfied with my modest climbing achievement, while my little brother scrambled higher and higher above me, hooting like a monkey. I admit to joy in knowing the stupid kid would never get down, but he always did, and I found some joy in that, too.

If you are buying, I will make you a deal you can't pass up. If you just take this beauty out for a joyride, you never need to bring her back. All I am asking for it is a little smile.

My Career as a Male Belly Dancer

Judy and I had been classmates since the third grade. We were seniors at Laramie High, and our class of '61 was putting on an all-school assembly. There would be solos and small ensembles of brave kids in band and choir, tap dancers, a silly skit or two, and a few rock-and-roll songs by the Imperials, our local garage band. It was nothing special, just a nice way to enjoy being seniors and have some fun.

Judy was doing the "Honey Bun" piece from the popular Broadway musical and motion picture *South Pacific*. I had seen the movie, laughing at the production number with Mitzi Gaynor in a sailor suit and Ray Walston as Honey Bun in a flowered skirt and bikini top. I asked Judy the day before the show to let me join her act. She didn't turn me down, but she probably wished she had.

It was a grand opportunity to display my unique and only performance talent. I could roll my stomach in a contraction and expansion of belly muscle that began at the sternum and proceeded in rolling waves to and from my waist. Nobody outside my family had ever seen me do this, and I was excited and not even a bit embarrassed to bring it to the public. Ray Walston could do it, too, but I was better.

I visited Woolworths and a grocery store to buy some colorful cotton yardage to pin around my waist, some cotton cord, and a nice, round coconut. With materials in hand, limited knowledge of coconuts, and absolutely no experience with brassieres, I proceeded.

Using some of Dad's tools, I cut the coconut in half, drilled the necessary holes, and assembled my new top. Trying it on, I discovered one weighty engineering problem. While I am sure the Maidenform people deal with all types of gravitational issues, I solved mine by eating the coconut, or enough of it that I had a light and balanced load hanging around my neck.

Felt-tip markers were a new product in the early sixties, and I found some colorful ones to tattoo my belly with a fine, steaming tugboat to ride the waves. I borrowed some of Mom's rouge to do my cheeks (the ones on my face).

All this I accomplished the night before the big show, leaving no opportunity for Judy and me to rehearse the number together. I had not even told her about my costume, and she had no inkling until I came in from the wing to meet her at the introduction of our act. I could see her taken aback, but let me tell you, Judy was a trouper. She danced and sang every note and word of "Honey Bun," and my belly kept the rhythm. I turned my butt to the audience when Judy arrived at the line, "I call her hips 'Twirly and Whirly,'" and each cheek performed on cue. We were magnificent, and so was Judy.

At our class reunion fifty years later, I briefly reminded Judy of our triumph. I am sure she had not thought about it for the six hundred months that had intervened, but she remembered and laughed, and that was the extent of our reminiscence. Looking back, I think we were each satisfied with our own performance that day and content to go our separate ways.

That was also the end of my career as a male belly dancer. I tried once for a revival, but the tattoo had faded and spread over too much poundage. Chippendales would not even talk to me. I have no regrets, but if I were to do it over again, next time I would buy a bigger coconut.

Football, Autumn Leaves, and Cinders

In writing of growing up in Laramie, I think of autumn, and mixes of aromas, sounds, and other sensations flood my memory and bring me back to a time that will never be again and maybe should never be missed but will.

Walk home with me today. It is a Saturday in early October 1953. We are ten years old, you and I, and we have spent the morning at the library at Fourth and Grand. It is a big, old building with an aroma of steam pipes, leather bindings, mildew, and magic lurking in its dusty stacks. I met Robin Hood there, and I believe to this day that Sherwood Forest smells like the Carnegie Public Library.

Feel the wind swirling through town. It's just chilly enough that you need a light jacket. Downtown bustled this morning with a thousand shoppers, but it's empty now on a Saturday afternoon because the stores have closed for the big Wyoming Cowboys game. You can already hear the stadium from anywhere in town with the boom of a cannon, the band playing "Ragtime Cowboy Joe," and a roaring crowd bigger than the whole population of Laramie.

We walk past the Church of St. Lawrence O'Toole, and our conversation lapses as we nod to acknowledge God's presence, as Monsignor taught us. But I wonder why we always walk a bit faster when we go by.

We amble down Grand to Second and then south to the Gambles store where we stop a minute to admire bicycles, Schwinn Phantoms, in the window. They are built like Buicks, complete with white sidewall tires and rocket ray headlights.

We are getting close to the tracks now as we turn west again on Garfield toward the footbridge. The railroad engines idling down below get so loud that you nearly have to plug your ears. Man! Can you smell the soot? Something about Laramie's altitude must make a train spew black smut that sticks to buildings for blocks around. It has to do with the lack of oxygen screwing up the combustion. We learned that in science class, remember?

From the top of the footbridge, we can see miles down the main line where a single bright headlamp looms larger than the locomotive it leads, putting the dot on an exclamation point formed by black smoke rising from her firebox. I feel the pinprick of a cinder in my eye from another big engine steaming in place down below. Your own tears won't wash out a cinder. Your mom or maybe your sister must gently remove it. Don't ever, ever let your brother do it.

Some days, this old footbridge gets to shaking with all the activity underneath. I saw U.P. on a railroad car. Ha, ha! Hey, no slugging!

Look at that building down there. They call it the roundhouse, but it is actually in the shape of an arc with a big old turntable in the center. I think they are going to run an engine out of the shops now, so let's stop and watch. What an amazing thing, railroad turntables. Boy! If I ever get to work on the railroad, I hope they give me the turntable job.

This is the workingman's part of town. Houses on the east side have brick and stucco. Tarpaper is apt to cover the houses over here. It's the melting pot of Laramie, but it's where I live, and it's where we learn to get along with different people. Maybe someday we will move uptown to a house that's actually big enough for our family, but gosh, I hope not too soon.

Can you smell the leaves piling up? They're dank underneath, but on top, they're just right for some wrasslin'. In a few blocks, we'll cut over to Spruce Street and down to my house.

Does your dad work on the railroad, too? My dad's out on his run now, but he'll get in this afternoon. He will want me to help rake the yard. Maybe we can walk down to the river before he gets home. It's right behind the house, but all you can see from our yard is willows. Mom will have some good stuff for us to eat. Do you like sloppy joes?

How to Iron a Shirt: A Bachelor's Primer

The price of getting dress shirts professionally done is pushing two dollars, and I have resolved that henceforth I shall do them myself. Two dollars indeed. I invite you to join my revolution, and I'm happy to help by sharing all I know about the ironing of shirts.

You probably have the equipment somewhere around your bachelor pad, but it's likely you will go buy it new anyhow. Adequate steam irons are available for about forty dollars, but a really good one and, face it, the one you think you must have, can cost up to a hundred. The ironing board will be about twenty bucks, and I recommend a can of spray starch for a couple dollars. If you iron even five shirts a week, you will recoup your investment in about three months.

Now that you are properly equipped, the first task is to set up the ironing board. Hold the apparatus laterally, reach across with your free hand, and feel for a lever under the other side. You may need to run your hand back and forth a couple times to find it. It may even turn out to be on your side, and you can check, but it takes a different motor skill.

If you cannot find it in the blind, rotate the board to a vertical position with the bottom facing you. If you are doing this in the dining room, as a bachelor naturally would, be careful of the chandelier. Now that you know where it is, turn the board away from you, and activate the lever.

I failed to mention, when squeezing the trigger on an ironing board in the vertical position, you should be at least four feet from anything else. If this advisement is too late, push the breakage aside for cleanup later. You are busy now.

The ironing board is now open. If you find it too high for comfort, you already know where the magic adjustor is. Reach over and push it. If the board collapses and you go with it, then you should not have been leaning on it. You will get it eventually, so keep trying.

The next step is to put on the cover. You can tell which way it goes by the shape, pointy end over pointy end. Better covers have a single draw cord, but the model you bought, you cheapskate, has strings along the length of the cover. These should be tied together in pairs under the surface. You can try to do this by feel, but blind knot tying is a talent uncommon to the male species, so you may have to turn the board over again, but for goodness sake, be careful this time. If you cannot get at least one pair of strings tied, paper clips will work for the time being, or, because it is you the bachelor, for the life of the ironing board.

Next, find the optimal placement for the ironing board. It should stand somewhere between you and an electrical outlet. If the outlet is behind you, the cord will ensnare your ankle and take you to the floor when you execute the grand lunge, the hot iron will land on your chest, and the board will follow.

With the apparatus erect and the iron plugged in, it is time to add distilled water. Did I not tell you to pick up distilled water? Sorry. You may substitute tap water but nothing else, even if does claim to be distilled. Set the iron to steam and the heat to max. You are ironing shirts, not frilly unmentionables, and anything short of hotter than Hades is unmanly.

The appliance will take time to warm up, so now you can go to the couch and catch a few minutes of that game. When you finally awaken in the middle of the night, the safety timer will have turned the iron off, and it will be cold again. Unplug it, and go to bed.

I have gone too long, so I will finish in a future episode. Then I will explain my ironing techniques, including the previously referenced grand lunge. In the meantime, leave the ironing board set up in your dining room. It makes a dandy buffet.

My Bucket List

The idea of making a list of things to do before you die is not new, but now it has a name, and the notion becomes more popular as we gain ground on the inevitable. My bucket list is typical, a mix of things I would like to do and places I would like to see.

This spring, I am going to New Orleans, Savannah, and Asheville. I will drive the Blue Ridge Parkway, and I might even see the Shenandoah Valley. My plans include Banff and Vancouver. Someday I will kiss the Blarney Stone.

There is a book waiting down deep in my bucket. It will probably be a collection of small pieces not much different or of more import than this, but if I can put a cover on it, I will call it a book.

There are some things, however, that I should just give up on. I will never become a telephone switchboard operator, nor have I hope of being an elevator operator. Any chance to be a copy boy at a big newspaper in the metropolis has dried up. There are no more typesetters at the newspaper either, and when was the last time you heard, "Call for Philip Morris", and what was that guy's job anyway?

It is too late to travel to Constantinople, Leningrad, Siam, or Ceylon. Saigon would have been interesting, but not as Ho Chi Minh City. I missed New Amsterdam by four centuries and Idlewild Airport by five decades. I have seen their successors, New York City and JFK Airport, but it's not the same.

I will draw from my bucket until I have kicked it, but the list will never be cleared because I keep finding new places and things to see and do. They say getting there is half the fun and the venture is more important than the achievement, but dreaming it up is even more fun.

On reflection, I should probably scratch traveling to Oz or, for that matter, becoming the Wizard of Oz. It is ironic because I am just reaching that age of silver and girth where I would make a very wonderful wizard. Are you listening, Hollywood?

9

THE DAY THE HOUSE BLEW UP

I grew up in an Irish Catholic family of seven children west of the tracks in Laramie and on the bank of the Laramie River. The floor plan of our house was a circuit, and a walk from room to room to room would soon return you to where you started.

When I was nine or ten, my parents undertook a remodeling to accommodate our burgeoning family. A new electric water heater was installed, large enough to support a family of nine. Even though it was adequate and modern, Dad soon had buyer's remorse. He knew the appliance was consuming rivers of electricity, and he checked the meter daily, sometimes more, extrapolating forecasts of huge bills. But even more than the financial consequences, Dad was sure the thing was destined to explode.

Mom must have been on an errand that summer afternoon because, if she had been home, things would have been calmer. We were active kids, and so it was unusual that we all happened to be indoors when Dad heard the first, foreboding hiss. "Good God Almighty! She's ready to blow! You kids get out of here! Now!"

The hiss grew to a roar, Dad got louder, and we all joined the cacophony, jumping around and yelling to and at no one in particular. We forgot where the doors were. We ran the course of our house, colliding with furniture and each other. We went through the hallway, through the front bedroom, through the living room, right past the front door, through the dining room, through the kitchen, past the back door, back into the hall, and around again, each of us seeking escape from Dad's frantic exhortations and certain doom.

We were still trapped inside and in pandemonium as the roar returned to a hiss and then to a whisper, trailing down the alley and up the next block along the Laramie River. The roar that nearly leveled 718 Spruce was merely the county, spraying for mosquitoes.

My Dad, a Character

He was a railroad man's railroad man, and by his estimation, that meant dressing in a railroad cap, a bandana, and bib overalls. Mom would regularly launder it all, blocking the cap and starching and ironing the overalls. It was a lot of work. After diesel engines replaced steam and he was no longer shoveling coal into a hot firebox, he no longer needed the protection of overalls. He may have been the last railroader in town to make the switch, but Mom finally got him into wash-and-wear work clothes by making it entirely his own idea.

He was born Daniel Emmett Knight. He was Emmett to his family, but he became better known as Mickey during his boxing career. Our guess is he had been billed on the fight cards as "The Fighting Mick," and the name stuck. He never legally changed it, but he hired out on the railroad as Michael Emmett Knight. That caused confusion when he retired, and it took an affidavit by his sister, our Aunt Josie, to get it straightened out with the Railroad Retirement Board.

He would regale us at the dinner table with tales of his childhood as the son of an Irishman on the Navajo Reservation in New Mexico. He would start with a humorous adventure of some sort but soon ramp up the stories, testing the credulity of the whole family of seven children. One frequent theme, told in a variety of ways, would reach its climax in an overturned outhouse. Mom said she could predict the tallness of the tale by the sparkle in his eye.

He refused the notion of travel by air. We learned why when he told my brother about once taking the dare of a barnstormer who came to town to give rides in the open cockpit of a sputtering flying machine. It was enough to make him promise the good God in heaven never to leave the ground again.

He kept that vow until he was seventy-eight and took a trip with Mom to Ireland after giving himself a dispensation to fly because it was a nice, safe Catholic tour. Coincidentally, on the very morning of the flight, there was breaking news of the crash of an Air India jet, ironically off the coast of Ireland. That terrible news was artfully kept from Dad, and the trip was a big success for them both.

Dad got along quite well with his father-in-law, a Methodist preacher, and they enjoyed each other's company. That is a story in itself because Grandpa was a Lincoln Republican who frowned on all the vices and Dad was a Roosevelt New Dealer, an Irish Catholic, a smoker, and not exactly dry. Perhaps the bond, beyond family itself, was that they shared an irreverent sense of humor and the ability to laugh at the high and mighty.

He was a lifelong student of history and politics and admired the eloquent speeches of Franklin Roosevelt and John Kennedy. With my brother, he watched the live broadcast of the "I Have a Dream" speech by Martin Luther King Jr., and when it was finished, Dad proclaimed it the greatest speech he had ever heard.

In 1969, the coach fired fourteen black players on the Wyoming Cowboys football team for asking permission to wear black armbands at a game with Brigham Young University in protest of Mormon racial policies of the time. Dad condemned the coach's action, probably too loudly, at a local watering hole crammed with loyal cowboys, barely escaping with his scalp.

Dad's friend, Joe Sanchez, worked as a hostler in the Laramie rail yards, operating locomotives to move cars around the freight yard but never taking the trains on the road. In the early forties, Dad was a griever for the union. The U.P. needed men for engine crews on the road, but they would not promote a Mexican or other minority employee. Dad risked his job by taking Joe's case to headquarters in Omaha, arguing Sanchez was the best employee in the yards and deserved the promotion. Well, he lost the battle, and he was nearly fired himself until Mr. Sanchez came to our house, thanked him for his support, and withdrew his application. By then, Dad was no longer the griever because the union was not too happy with him either.

We fondly recall our dad as a character, but we will never forget the character of the man.

Are We There Yet?

One of us in our Buick full of little Knights was sure to ask, "Are we there yet?" It is one of the first rhetorical questions of children everywhere, a bladder issue, and a tactful way of telling the old man to step on it. Our dad always understood and probably shared the urgency. We would sense a positive response by way of a bit more acceleration and we didn't need to ask the question again.

I've been thinking the last few days about doing an essay on the question as a metaphor of life. The answer, as I would reveal it, is always soon but never yes because the meaning of life is in the voyage and destinations are but waypoints.

I believe Frederick Bonfils, the cofounder of the *Denver Post*, captured this idea when he wrote, "There is no hope for the satisfied man." He had it carved in stone over the entrance to the *Post*'s editorial offices.

I remember long drives with my children. I would answer their requests for ETA with the stock "It won't be long now" and then sing an irritating verse of "peas, peas, peas, peas, eating goober peas." They got the joke but had to squeeze the old muscle down tighter, and their suppressed giggling just made it worse for them. I would redeem myself by finding a place to pull over. Having only sons meant I could be less selective about pit stops.

I have told the story before of one particular such moment. I had taken the boys on a pleasure and learning trip through the Midwest. We called it our "Mark Twain, Baseball, and Hot Dogs Tour," and it involved fireflies, a visit to Hannibal, a couple of overnights in St. Louis to see the Cardinals, a roundabout drive through the Ozarks, and then to Kansas City for a Royals game and a day at one of their great amusement parks.

While driving through the Ozarks, we encountered a length of highway that went for miles in a close series of small hills quickly rising and sharply falling. Each drop left our tummies hanging in space and the boys rolling in laughter. They were having a wonderful time of it, and I was getting credit for a brilliant piece of driving when Robert, then four, suddenly and urgently had to pee.

I eased the car to the edge of the road. Thomas, seven years the elder, hopped out, and as he opened the rear door for his brother, the car began listing to the right. What I had perceived as solid shoulder was only dense vegetation, mowed on a plane with the pavement. The boys scrambled to safety just as a concerned Missouri game warden pulled up behind our vehicle, which was now off level by twenty degrees. It was a minor tilt really, but it felt treacherous and looked worse.

The warden coached me back to terra firma. I got the boys back in and belted in their seats, and we proceeded quietly, grateful for our friendly warden and guardian angel. The boys dozed off, and I enjoyed the rolling green scenery for quite some time before I heard a sleepy plea from the backseat, "Daddy, are we there yet?" I selected a nice, safe turnout, and we were all relieved.

This essay seems to have gone on a couple detours, and before you ask the obvious, the answer is no, but we will be there soon. Perhaps Gertrude Stein was pondering the famous question when, after traveling to Oakland in search of her childhood home and finding it gone, she wrote, "There is no there there."

And that, my friends, is what we find as we pull into the driveway at the end of this rambling piece. There is no there here either.

The Personality Transplant

It struck me in reflecting on a challenge to write on the topic of personality that perhaps I could use one myself. As it is, I might as well describe the charisma of a bat in a cave. Unlike the bat, I don't provoke comment when I hang from my toes, and I can't see or hear bugs in the dark. So you see my dilemma. I need a transplant.

I know I should just write about the person I am, but the fellow I want to profile is one who radiates, so I spent the weekend poring through entertainment and personality magazines looking for famous radiators as potential role models. I found some interesting ones, but they all seem to come with drawbacks, the biggest one being the need for fame and the inability to handle it when they get it. The people in *People* are very good looking, but while I don't deny I could use a facelift and some general rearrangement, I'm really in the market only for a new personality.

It looks like my best chance will be to design one of my own. The core trait I would adapt is that of an extrovert. It would give me the capacity to drop in on any social or business event and work the room. I would sling terms like "doll" and "babe," and my hands would be everywhere and anywhere. I would be unconcerned for other people's space because I would be the most important person there. I would interrupt conversations by the dozen but finish none because I would always be flitting to the next.

I might add also the dimension of adventurer. After all, if I'm going to do the talking, I might as well fill it with stories of daring escapades to share with those who will be drawn to my radiance. Maybe I should add a hint of bad boy. It is said that men with such a strain fascinate women. Is it the dark and dangerous side or perhaps the charm of unpredictability? Oh my, this is going to be fun.

Now I have to consider how to get the transplant done. Are there psychologists who will do this sort of thing? Can a hypnotist do it? How about acupuncture? Is there an Earl Scheib on Colfax offering cheap personality paint jobs?

My instinct tells me, besides designing my own, I will have to install the new personality by myself. The costs will be not in what I desire to become but in what I must give up to get there.

Maybe I should reconsider this whole project. After all, I do like being in small social situations, and I will even attend large events if I can find a quiet space in the corner for a nice conversation with those nearby. The pleasure and value I get from being with other people comes from what I hear, not from what I say.

If being an extrovert means I must work the room, I guess I don't want the job. And frankly, while I enjoy the company of others, I am also happy in solitude. A little introversion and a little introspection while hanging in the bat cave may make a personality too boring to write about, but then again, who's writing?

A Morning at the Museum

It is a crisp winter morning, and bison are there before me on a high point overlooking Rocky Flats. A bull idly watches a cow rolling on the snowy ground, heavily insulated in her furry coat. I can almost hear her grunts of appreciation as she scratches her back on the friendly, rough terrain. A jackrabbit in white winter camouflage stands alert among the beasts. It is his domain for the moment, but he is about to spring off to a new one under cover as his cocked ears detect the shriek of a golden eagle soaring high above.

I was there as a toddler and many more times growing up, and I made visits with my boys when they were children, too. So I decided this morning to renew my acquaintance with the wonderful Denver Museum of Nature and Science.

The building, dating back to 1908, was expanded in 1940 and then again in 1968, 1983, and most recently in 2014. It is the largest natural history museum in the Western United States, full of everything from musk oxen to Mars rovers. To see and appreciate it all takes days of wandering and wondering.

Wings are dedicated to space exploration, mummies, gems and minerals, good health, insects and butterflies, birds, and dinosaurs. This morning, I am concentrating on my favorite, the grand dioramas of wildlife from all over the world artistically set in their natural habitats. I will sit on the benches and imagine them coming to life.

I move to another display, and I am mesmerized by a mountain lion hovering over a white-tailed deer she has carried home to her babies, a magnificent dinner for this sunny afternoon in the foothills. Her four spotted kittens rush to the feast. They will never know their father, who left Mom after a brief courtship in the manner of his dad and fathers before him. Descriptive museum signs full of such information are everywhere but go mostly unread in favor of the riveting scenes portrayed.

A diorama of bighorn sheep in the Tarryall area of Colorado's South Park shows these kings in all their glory. It is fascinating to see the model of a cloven hoof, spread and pointed with inner pads, rubbery to grip narrow, steeply inclined surfaces, and soft to absorb the impact as the ram leaps from protrusion to precipice below, sometimes dropping twenty feet.

Disease decimated the bighorns of Colorado in the late nineteenth century and first four decades of the twentieth when finally a new herd was introduced in the Tarryall Mountains in 1940. The healthy sheep we now see in Rocky Mountain National Park, Mount Evans, and other parts of the state descended mostly from that Tarryall herd.

Elk with handsome racks bark in a grove, enjoying the tasty, white skin of the plentiful aspen. Barking doesn't directly harm the tree, but there is a risk of infection as it heals. Every trunk in the grove displays a history of black scars. If you push the button below the diorama, you hear an elk bugle, and shortly, another bull answers, eagerly taking the challenge to a duel. Push it a couple more times, and you are ready to lock horns yourself.

As the halls fill with young families, I enjoy the enthusiasm of children as they dart to and fro, their eyes briefly catching a snake and then an owl in a corner of some diorama. Their attention spans seem so brief that I really can't put myself in their place. I suppose I was that way too as a four-year-old at the museum, but if so, how did I gain such complete impressions in my memory of grizzlies, polar bears, walruses, and turtles? A lot must register in those nanoseconds.

My trips to the Denver Museum of Nature and Science are too infrequent. Perhaps I should spend more of my free mornings and afternoons here, walking with dinosaurs, squinting at sparkling minerals and gems upstairs, and exploring outer space in the inner spaces. The stars of the Gates Planetarium will remind me of sleeping under the Wyoming sky. All of that is waiting, but I suspect every future trip will still include a stroll among my awesome dioramas.

OUT STANDING IN MY FIELD

It is a tired old cliché of a joke, but it describes the situation, and I use it unabashedly as it was the one moment in my life where I may lay claim to the distinction. It was a summer morning in 1953. I was nine going on ten and out standing in my field. It was lollygagging actually, and my mind was anywhere but on the important job at hand, which was that of Little League outfielder. A major feature of lollygagging is that your reflexes become sleepy and difficult to summon when called upon.

The screaming of teammates startled me out of my reverie, and my eyes finally focused on the vision of an orb flying in from an indeterminate place. With myopia, then undiagnosed, and the associated lack of depth perception, I couldn't judge its distance or how much time I had left, but it was close enough that I knew it was a baseball and it was about to arrive.

My choices, swiftly considered, were to fall into a fetal position, dodge, turn and run, or bat the object away to protect my precious Irish noggin. Choosing the latter, I shut my eyes, drew my hands up with my glove turned outward in a paddle position, and heard the smack of leather meeting leather.

I will leave you to ponder whether I made the game-ending catch, clinching the championship for my team, and established my fame or whether the ball dribbled from my glove, allowing runners to score, the season to end, and my infamy confirmed.

Whatever you conclude, I will tell you this, and I declare it loudly and happily. It was the last time I have ever been caught out standing in my field.

Mr. Manners on Elevator Etiquette

This columnist gets questions about proper comportment in and around elevators and takes note of a rising level of complaints about rude behaviors. It is yet another mandate for your wise Mister Manners to set rules and bring order to a common part of your daily lives. First the mail:

Dear Mister Manners: My wife was furious with me this morning when I bowed to a comely young woman who approached the elevator we were about to board. I smiled to the lass and gestured for her to enter first. I stepped in and smiled again. The wife glowered and followed me in, her posterior briefly interrupting the operation of the doors, but they finally won out. Mildred is not speaking to me now. What did I do wrong?

Signed, Wally from Wiggins

Dear Wally: You should have pressed the "close door" button before the missus could squeeze in. Two's company. Three's a crowd. I hope you enjoyed the trip despite the extra baggage.

Dear Mister Manners: I am a woman of matronly proportion and was downtown a few days ago for an appointment on the eighteenth floor of one of the big bank buildings. There were a number of us taking the elevator up. I was the first one there and the first one on, and thus I was entitled to be the first one off.

I rightfully took the front center position to mark and hold my priority all the way to my destination on eighteen. The other passengers worked around me and got in. The elevator opened at sixteen, and a cur of a young man shoved past with an "Excuse me, ma'am," as if those words should prompt me to defer. Well, the

closing door barely missed my foot when I kicked him in the ass. Don't you agree he acted unmannerly?
Signed, Dee from Denver

Dear Dee: I thank you because the impression you left on my backside that morning set me to thinking about systems that would allow people like you to go up in a building without having to share your conveyance with anyone else. I believe the best opportunity is something I am calling a personal elevation device, and it involves a helmet and a cannon.

The difficulties will be its open-air nature and the labor costs. Self-service cannons must yet be developed, and the engineers will need to be skilled because there are precise calculations concerning weight, trajectory, windage, and gunpowder. Nets at each floor will make a good landing system and will work nicely when you are going down.

This venture is the ticket to my fortune, and someday I can kiss this Mister Manners gig good-bye. Investment opportunities are available.

The Kiddy Show

I was in high school when I landed my first job as an usher at the Fox Theater in Laramie. I was quite the flashlight handler from the beginning, and soon I was qualified to substitute for the doorman, pour sodas, sell popcorn, man the ticket booth, change the marquee, and do just about anything at the movies but run the projector.

Our manager feared children but loved to watch them buy tickets and line up with money for popcorn, so he scheduled a series of kiddy shows for Wednesday afternoons in the summer. I was to be the master of ceremonies and the theater's playbill in that morning's *Laramie Boomerang* proclaimed, "Uncle Dennis on Stage!"

I prepared my debut with the fervor of the ham I was then and still am. We had lined up a double feature with lots of cartoons and a fifteen-minute break in the middle for my stage appearance. I bought prizes from the dime store, things like jump ropes and paddleballs. My official green usher uniform with fringed golden epaulets made me look like a teenaged Captain Kangaroo, and I even wrote a theme song, which I have never forgotten but will spare you today.

Laramie High, like high schools everywhere, had an association for the athletes. Ours was the L Club, and as a journalism student, I reported on their athletic exploits, envying all the while their popularity with girls. I was not thinking of them at all on the day of my debut as Uncle Dennis, but as it happened, that was just the day the club had picked to treat children from the orphanage to an afternoon at the movies.

We opened the theater with a line going down the block, and, as they entered, I conducted what I made into a ceremonious process of greeting each child and collecting his or her ticket. Imagine the sinking feeling that hit me when, at some point in the progression, every member of the football team showed up, each with an orphan in tow. Bravado abandoned me, and butterflies rose in a sense of pending humiliation. The rest of my high school career was doomed.

The first feature ran barely an hour, and then some cartoons played while I fretted and sweated in a corner behind the curtain. Finally, the lights came on and there before me was a large, illuminated void, demanding to be filled. A reception of five hundred happy children greeted me as I took the stage, but I saw in the crowd only gleefully smug faces of the defensive line, the offensive line, assorted backfields, and the star quarterback. They were taking it all in, every gruesome detail of it, and I was terrified.

I did not know whether to sing my theme song or not, but I swallowed and did it anyway. I did it badly, but I did it. I brought kids on stage to play games for prizes, and everyone, even, I think, the football team, had a good time. My allotted time ran out, and I was happy to skip my planned second song, a sing-along to "Do-Re-Mi" from *The Sound of Music*.

Summer passed with movies, cartoons, contests, and Uncle Dennis on stage every week. My senior year at Laramie High began, football season started, and from the L Club, I got the very best response I could have hoped for, which was zilch. Maybe it was because they realized that none of them to that time ever actually had any more courage than I did that day.

The manager of the Fox decided to continue kiddy shows on into the school year with me on stage every Saturday, and although I never reprised my performance of that theme song, I still have not forgotten the lyrics. It has been fifty-three years, but I believe I could be doing Uncle Dennis on Stage even today if the Army hadn't called.

THE DAY THE MUSIC SLOWED: A LOVE AFFAIR

Paul and I were born in early September 1943, he one day before me. Our fifth birthdays fell a week after the cutoff for enrollment in the Laramie Public Schools, so our mothers, each believing her own progeny prodigious and ready for the world of kindergarten, went to the school board and got an exception that allowed us to enter that year.

I went to Lincoln School, and Paul attended another across town. It happened that we were both from Catholic families, so when the new St. Laurence School opened four years later, Paul and I were in third grade, together again for the first time since our days in the maternity ward. We were both in the short percentile of physical development, so we would likely have been among the smallest boys in our class even if we had not been pressed into school a year before our time. This was clearly double jeopardy, and our mothers and the school board should have known better.

As we entered the sixth grade, the nun who ran the music program thought it would be clever and visually cute to recruit short little Paul to play the big bass drum in the school orchestra and short little Denny to play the same thing in the school band. That instrument dwarfed us both.

Paul stayed in the orchestra only through the sixth grade, as he was much the wiser of us by virtue of being a day older. He realized he was being exploited for a teacher's private gag, so he quit. I was appointed to keep the joke going and play in both band and orchestra. By then, my curls peaked and peeked just over the top of the drum if I stood straight, but I couldn't because I had to lean to one side in order to see the director.

In the eighth grade, our orchestra had an opportunity to go down to Colorado for a citywide parochial music concert at the Denver Auditorium. We had rehearsed a group of classical compositions, and as we took the stage, I was pretty convinced we were the best orchestra on the entire program and would surely get a standing ovation.

My friend Kathy was the student conductor, and I relied on the rhythm of her wand to get me through to the end of each piece without missing a beat. And it did for the better part of our evening. The climax of our performance was Schubert's famous *Unfinished Symphony*, and I came very near to making certain that we did not finish it either.

As Kathy led us into the powerful middle of the symphony, a part with lots of my bass drum filling the hall, I saw, just below and to the left of her graceful baton, the most beautiful sight in the entire auditorium.

She was in the seventh row, a thirteen-year-old vision in golden tresses, a button nose, and a brand-new figure, a big city girl for sure. Our eyes met in one of those moments when the world slows to let you soak it in. Well, what actually slowed was my drum, drifting into a languorous love song unrelated to the performance at hand.

Suddenly the corner of my eye caught sight of a rapidly twitching baton signifying the conductor's panic in the face of a train wreck. Kathy had finally broken my trance, and she skilfully pulled me back into tempo with the orchestra to glide in harmony and rhythm right through the rest of the symphony. We finished it for Mr. Schubert quite beautifully.

It was our big ending. We got our standing ovation and took an extra bow. I took another for myself and looked for the pretty girl in the seventh row, hoping to take one more for her. She was gone, but to this day, I have never forgotten her and our brief teenage romance, which was entirely contained and remains today locked in the memory of those wonderful eight seconds when the music slowed.

THERE OUGHT TO BE A LAW

Nothing is worse than going into the queue, or as we, the victims call it, being put on terminal hold. "Your call is important to us ... We value your business ... Your call will be answered in the order in which it was received." We hear a few bars of the same tiring song and puffery about the company, all repeating in a loop.

I propose legislation that would ban outright the diabolical practice of putting customers in a queue and a system of fines to enforce it. My law would also require every chief executive in America to call anonymously his or her own customer service lines on a weekly basis to experience personally whatever torture his or her organization is perpetrating. This would apply but not be limited to merchants, bankers, gadget makers, and the Postmaster General.

A couple weeks ago, I ran into a problem setting up my new Blu-ray player. After the man on the help line spent some time tripping over the question and putting me on hold several times, always with the same loop to consult his script, he came back for a final time to advise me that Samsung's servers were down for maintenance and I should try again in twenty-four hours. I know that, before I said a word, he could sense I was levitating and ready to hit the ceiling.

"That is unacceptable," I informed the agent, who spoke in broken English from some remote corner of the globe. I demanded to speak to a supervisor. Using the vernacular of customer service, that meant I was demanding to be escalated and my call was routed off to Corporate.

I then found myself back on terminal hold, but this time with no loop of platitudes and commercials, not even bad music. I waited in abject silence for thirty minutes before a couple clicks came through the receiver and a cheerful recording kicked in to announce how important my call was but imploring me to please call back during normal business hours.

I had wasted an hour of my Saturday morning on Samsung. It was time I had expected to be recording on my brand-new Samsung device streams of whatever drivel I could find. I put down the phone in a stream of my own drivel, profane, mindless, and satisfying. I did not intend to wait twenty-four hours to commence another bout of bad customer service, so I took a break, had a beer, and started the installation process again from scratch.

Magically, someone upstream had rebooted Samsung's servers, and my new Blu-ray device went online without a hitch in something less than a minute. It brings to mind the snippet of a song, and now I am trying to remember the rest of that tune that goes, "Samsung Blu, Everybody Knows One."

Summer Vacation

No more pencils,
No more books,
No more teachers' dirty looks.

I learned that ditty when I graduated from kindergarten, and I recited it annually for twelve more years. I knew there were among us the teacher's pets, girls, mostly, who loved school so much that they couldn't possibly have uttered those words, but I shouted them with glee, and I had plenty of company. It would take me another half century to learn there is more to the poem:

When the teacher rings the bell,
Drop your books and run like hell.

There is yet a different version, and it rhymes just as nicely. It would have me drop my pencils in the well, and tell the teachers to go to, well, someplace.

Of course we couldn't drop our books and run like hell without one last teacher's dirty look, suggesting we make our summer vacation an educational experience, spending it in the library or going to museums. It was fair warning that, when September came, I would be expected to produce a report on something I did that was worthwhile during those three lovely intervening months.

But writing was far from my mind when I was climbing over fences just for the joy of ignoring perfectly functioning gates, or collecting salamanders in the morning, just to release them in the afternoon. I wasn't concerned about any essay when my little brother Jim and I decided to ride our one-speed bicycles all the way to the Snowy Range, thirty miles to the west. We made it three whole miles, all uphill and into the wind, before we turned back. And for some reason that I am sure is scientific, the ride home was also uphill and into the wind. It took us the better part of the day, but we were wiser for the effort.

I wasn't thinking of a report when my brother Jerry, six years my elder, a responsible young man of fourteen and trustee of our Grandpa's twenty-two rifle, took me on a hunting expedition up the Laramie River. We brought along with us sack lunches and two bottles of pop, but no church key to open them with. When we discovered the problem at lunch time, Jerry cleverly set the bottles upright and shot the caps off. It seemed a neat solution, but he was smart enough to realize our sodas now contained shards of glass. I thirstily offered that we could just spit out the glass, but I was denied. My baloney sandwich was tasty, I thought, although a little dry without the wash down of that beautiful grape Nehi sitting over there so forlornly.

Now I am seventy years old, and I have finally gotten around to writing about what I really did on my summer vacation. I will summarize by telling you I did a lot of things and, while it didn't involve libraries or a museum, it certainly was an education.

HOME ECONOMICS 101 FOR BOYS

Mrs. Jones, one of the home economics teachers at Laramie High, persuaded the school administration to let her offer a special course in the subject for boys. She was the young wife of an athletic trainer at the University of Wyoming and, as a couple, they also managed a residence hall for the athletes.

I believe it was her experience and empathy for males newly away from home and mother that prompted her to teach the course. She would give lessons and experiences in the arts of attaching buttons, ironing garments, cooking on the stove and in the oven, determining nutrition, planning a household budget, shopping for groceries, and more. We would even bake a cake from scratch, not out of a box.

I saw the class offering as a chance to grab some needed credits and snag an A to buttress my sad grade point average. The fact it added an extra hour to my school day at seven in the morning was not daunting, so I was first in line to register, figuring I would have an easy time of it. Surely, I had the genes of my mother who had a college degree in home economics and was a creative homemaker and the mother of seven.

The first unit was on the ironing of shirts, a skill Mom had taught me well. I was and still am so good at it that I even wrote a recent white paper on the topic. I breezed through the unit, and Mrs. Jones held me up as a shining example for the fellows who could not tell their placket from their buttonhole. I was definitely in for an A, maybe an A-plus. I did well through most of the other units, too. I had learned to cook at home and generally understood how to follow sequence, measure, stir, and use a timer.

For the cooking and baking unit, we were divided into teams and assigned to the available ranges and ovens in the classroom. All I can say now is the other three fellows on my team must have been idiots. How else would you explain what happened on the day we made our yellow cake from a scratch recipe? My sleepy team took too long that morning mixing the ingredients and getting the batter evenly divided into pans and into the oven. Suddenly the bell rang, and Mrs. Jones shooed us along to our next classes, telling us the girls in the eight o'clock hour would take our cake out when it was done.

I went anxiously through my next two periods. Then at ten, I ducked out of study hall to check on the outcome. On arrival I was greeted by laughing sophomore girls and two large, flat, cookie-like things at my workstation. Mrs. Jones was not pleased and ordered me to round up my team to come back after school and clean the residue from the bottom of the oven.

I do not remember my final grade for Boys Home Economics but it didn't have a plus in it. In reporting this story, I have done some reading on baking chemistry and the effects of baking powder and have figured out there must have been a mix up of teaspoons and tablespoons by some genius among us. Certainly, it was not I.

Searching for the Meaning of Life

What is the meaning of life? So far, I have been up to just about any writing challenge. But the meaning of life? Like any modern fellow, I googled it and got a long answer that started with Plato and meandered through the philosophies, Western and Eastern, from cynicism to hedonism to nirvana.

Many highfalutin thinkers have told us how to live, chase our dreams, matter, count for something, impart life to others and pass along what wisdom we manage to acquire along the way.

The meaning of life is central to the world's religions. Pope Benedict in 2009 said, "Life is not just a succession of events or experiences: it is a search for the true, the good and the beautiful." Buddhists teach life has meaning only if it is understood as a stepping-stone to an enlightenment in which the self escapes from worldly concerns.

Priests and philosophers tell us how to live, but they seem never to get to a conclusive definition of the meaning of life, so I moved on from Google to ask my new friend, Siri, about it. Siri is a digital personal assistant on my smartphone who can take instructions and answer queries in a pleasant voice. She will lead me to the nearest drugstore, put an appointment on my calendar, or take me to lunch.

I asked Siri to tell me the meaning of life, not once but three times. She responded in various ways. First, it was, "I can't answer it now, but give me time to write a long play in which nothing happens." The second time it was, "Try to be nice to people, avoid eating fat, read a good book every now and then, get some walking in, and try to live in peace and harmony." Her final answer humored me but was but satire, "All evidence to date suggests it's chocolate."

What I have learned so far about the meaning of life is that nobody has it figured out, that is, except maybe Fred the barber. I took my straggly mane and beard to Fred, hoping for an epiphany and a trim.

"What'll it be, Mac?" was the greeting as he offered the chair, summarily ignoring, if he heard it at all, my direction as he wrapped my neck, draped my body, and proceeded to whack to his own design. Indeed, it was his bullheaded contrariness, what I took to be Fred's unfettered view of life and existence, that led me to his counsel.

"Want me to get them nose hairs?" was another rhetorical pleasantry as he was going after them regardless.

Then I screwed up my courage and propounded my big question. There was a pause, a long, slow one.

"What the hell?" roared Fred. "The meaning of life?" He seemed to levitate over me, punctuating space with scissors and comb. "The meaning of life? Life is what happens when you're sweeping up the cuttings, Mac. There ain't no meaning of life. Hell, people been trying to answer that one for a million years, and they ain't got it right. I ain't never been asked before you come in here, and you ain't gonna get no philosophy outta me now. Better take that one to the bishop, Mac."

He snipped and clipped and finished me up in an irritated flurry, flashing a mirror for two seconds to let me review his work. The haircut was just okay, but I was happy because Fred had actually helped me solve the enigma for myself.

The meaning of life is to search for the meaning of life. I gave him a ten-dollar tip.

I'm an Old Cowhand

The topic is cows, and I can handle it just as well as anything else I've ever written about. I know which end of the bovine moos, and if ever I become a dairy man, I will study up on the other parts.

I can share one tidbit I happen to have. Have you ever noticed and wondered about the short piece of heavy chain suspended from a post in a typical cow pasture? Well, that, my friends, is old bossy's back scratcher. You usually see the apparatus near a water tank and a block of salt.

In fact, I actually do have some experience with the species. Many years ago, I was a guest on a farm that happened to have a herd of fifty or sixty cattle. To pay for my supper I was pressed into service to help move the herd from one pasture to another. It was not hard work because, when the cattle saw us coming across the field, they rounded themselves up in front of the gate to their next paradise. I only needed fancy footwork, if you get my drift, and if I did not have it, you would have gotten my drift for days.

Maybe it was the classic grass-is-greener mentality that drove them to the gate, but I am not sure cows even have a mentality. It was probably the same Pavlovian reaction I have to a sizzling T-bone.

When we got organized, our trail boss opened the gate, and the first four cows took four steps each into the new green pasture, stopped, and commenced to graze leisurely. Plugging up behind them was a hungry, angry, demanding bovine traffic jam.

We each carried braided whips, which we brandished unpersuasively to get them doggies moving. I heard cussing here and there, but I did not want to be a copycat, and besides, I was a rookie and not yet fully conversant with the subtleties of the wrangler lexicon.

I do not think there was a single cowboy hat among the humans on the drive, but there were a couple of sweaty green John Deere caps, which leant some authenticity. My own cap was a clean blue thing without even a logo I got at the drugstore. I tried to make up for it with some spitting, but it left my mouth dry.

Maybe we did not have horses and lassos, and there wasn't the whooping and hollering on the scale of the Chisholm Trail, but it was a cattle drive nonetheless. And while the sum total of my experience in that occupation, perhaps an hour, is not enough to put on a résumé if I'm ever invited to a cocktail party in Manhattan, I'll drop it in. "Why that reminds me, ma'am, of my days punching cows out in Colorado. Yup."

LET 'ER BLOW

We say rain brings pennies from heaven, and we dream of white Christmases, but I've never heard anyone sing, "Let it blow, let it blow, let it blow." Nobody likes the wind, but wherever you live, it's inevitable.

The windiest big city in the United States is Boston with an average annual wind speed of 12.3 miles per hour. Following are Oklahoma City, Buffalo, Milwaukee, and Dallas. The metropolis that claims to be *the* Windy City, Chicago, is way down at twelfth on the list.

Even Boston's ambient wind speed pales when compared to Dodge City with an average of 13.9, according to the US Climatic Data Center. On the other end of the scale, my reading says the most tranquil big city in America, by average, is Phoenix, but even that town is known to suffer wind gusts of up to a hundred miles per hour.

I cannot tell you the climate numbers for Rawlins, Wyoming, but it is the single windiest place I have ever lived. It is a rough and tough prison town, but its main claim to infamy is wind. I was sent there for a couple years back in the sixties when I had embarked on a career in retail management. I thought the incessant wind made it the single grouchiest place in America, and I do not think my finally blowing the burg made it any more congenial.

My intent for this piece, however, is not to damn the wind but to celebrate it. An old expression tells us it is an ill wind that blows nobody good. It is faint praise, but it's a start, so let's ramp it up with some real bluster.

The same wind that slows a jetliner to near hover speed while keeping it safely lifted in an airfoil will boost a plane cruising in the opposite direction to its destination well ahead of its ETA.

Winds that drop welcome snow over ski areas in January roar down the slopes to become the Chinooks that carry balmy temperatures to Denver in the winter. But if you are on the Sixteenth Street Mall, better hang on to your hat.

A crafty sailor scorns the wind that blows against him by tacking his vessel right into and through its powerful face. However, when breezes are idled, so too is the sailboat.

Without the wind, Don Quixote would have found no worthy opponent in tilting at the broad, slowly churning windmills of La Mancha. Imagine him today challenging giant farms of wind turbines atop towers ten, twenty, even thirty stories high, harnessing the wind to supply electricity for our cities.

All the while, back in Denver on the mall, a passing breeze raises a skirt and lifts the spirits of girl watchers. That, my friend, is no ill wind. Let 'er blow!

My Favorite Animal Family

They are an adaptable species, populating all climates and continents. They have an incredible range, and some individual members are known to travel back and forth across vast territories, often from continent to continent and even around the earth. You will see them scaling the highest peaks and cavorting in the depths of the ocean.

Most are carnivorous and employ many ways to vanquish and feast on other animals, yet others shun meat to subsist on fruits and vegetables. Choices in diet can be wide because of their dental structure, with canines for the ripping and tearing of meat and vegetable, incisors for biting, and molars for chewing and grinding. Most partake of a mix of flesh and vegetable, seeming to crave a variety of both.

They come in many colors and shades. Their manes may be short or long and may vary from yellows and whites to reds, blacks, and browns. Recently, younger specimens have been spotted in parrot-like purples and greens that appear to be evolutionary mutations, as it is rare to find such adaptations in more mature members of the species.

Like the common house fly and just as ubiquitous, they are known to spread disease, pestilence, and mayhem. They tend to colonize and often struggle with each other for domain, forging powerful alliances and battling to the death for territory and power.

It is commonly held that they mate for life, and many pairs do, but they are fickle, and often their relationships become confused, entangled, or angry, and the partnerships terminate. They seem quite jealous and possessive, and even after family units dissolve, uneasy relationships seem to linger for years.

Yet, my favorite animals can be curious, charming, and attractive. They are quite social and frequently share their habitats with other species, particularly canines and felines. They arrange their plumages to attract mates. Unlike most other species, members of both genders preen, posture, and often employ melodious vocalizations to promote and advance attachments. Chirping and cooing are an attractive part of their lexicon, but they grunt and growl as well. Flirting couples try combinations of all the above.

Their offspring are reared in a variety of ways, with most growing up in a protected and nourishing environment that continues until they reach maturity or even longer. Others seem to suffer from neglect or abandonment from early in life.

The members of my favorite animal family are often discouraging and frustrating, disappointing, irritating, frightening, and maddening. Yet they can be joyful, captivating, and entertaining. For a real good look at them, I suggest you go to any zoo in the world. In fact, I hope you will join me for a visit this afternoon to the Denver Zoo where I plan to sit on a park bench and just watch them roam and do all the crazy and silly things they, my favorite animals, the humans, do.

Dad and the Buick Woody

As often as I reflect on that day, I will never resolve what made Dad decide to paint the old car copper. Over the years, I have thought it might have been spring's gentle wakening of a winter daydream, but it might instead have sprung from an encounter with a wee drop of Old Crow.

It must have been about 1955. I was twelve and third in our family of seven kids growing up in Laramie. In a brood that large, there are not many times when a boy can spend hours alone with his dad, so if for no other reason, it was a special day for me.

Our venerable 1941 Buick Woody station wagon was no longer serving as the family's primary car. Her fenders and hood, originally a deep maroon, had faded to an irregular pink in the unfiltered sun of our high Wyoming plains, and the varnish on her wooden sides was about gone. But she ran fine and still held utility as a second car for our big family.

I did not know what was afoot that morning when Dad took me with him to Laramie Basin Hardware. He was not sure how much it would take, but after consulting with the proprietor, he bought the store's entire inventory of copper spray paint, four cans, with a promise they would take back what he did not need.

Parked in a shady spot south of the house, we took turns shaking the first can according to directions until the metal ball rattled. Imagine my excitement as Dad approached the car, aligned the nozzle, took aim at the prescribed distance, and pushed the button, creating on the swell of the left front fender a large coppery blob, surrounded by an oily blotch, going nowhere in particular but not staying in one place either.

Dad said nothing—not to me, not to the car, and not to the paint—but I knew he was at one of life's crossroads. Would he try to wipe off the mess and take the remaining cans back to the store, or would he spray on? Would another press of the nozzle mitigate the damage or merely embellish it? Would invoking the help of the Archangels save him from the wrath of Mom?

Courageously, he squeezed the nozzle again and then again, taking broader strokes until the can ran empty with only a patch painted. He had already passed the point of no return, and soon he exhausted the remaining cans on the same fender, still unfinished.

So we returned to the store, hoping a new shipment had arrived in the ninety minutes since we cleaned them out. Laramie Basin Hardware was still out of copper, had none on order, and was about the sorriest damned outfit Dad had ever dealt with. We went to every other place in town, even Woolworths, and bought out the town, amassing a box full of several different brands of spray paints, each claiming to be copper.

Dad's vision of a shiny copper Buick had dimmed, and he narrowed his scope to painting just the steel body parts, the fenders and hood. When it became obvious the various brands and dye lots would produce tones from rust to orange to gold, sometimes even copper, he tried to blend the variations and make them part of the esthetic. There was not much further dialog, but I could sense his urgency to finish the awful job and hide it in the alley before Mom came home. I stayed with him to the end.

I've forgotten how many cans of paint we sprayed that day, but not the result, a coppery 1941 Buick station wagon that shimmered in the bright Wyoming sun. It shimmered when it was cloudy. It shimmered in the moonlight. Lord, how it shimmered.

Mom and my big sister Maureen refused ever again to be seen in the vehicle, but the rest of us took to it after Dad varnished the wood and painted the trim pieces turquoise. Eventually, Dad and one of his cronies converted our Woody into a fishing car. They removed the backseat and installed a trap door, making a cache for over limit fish, safe from the game warden. But that's a different story.

Just Kidding

I confess to being a kidder by nature. Pulling legs is part of my normal interaction with society, and few are immune. It is not unusual for me to leave guests at a social occasion listing fore or aft with pulled legs. I have done it to parents, siblings, spouse and issue, lady friends, coworkers, teachers, clerics, politicians, storekeepers, and librarians.

I suppose I am splitting hairs when I admit to being a pathological kidder but not a liar. Mom told me once she could tell when I was lying because my nose wiggled and my voice cracked, so I avoid that activity. When I am kidding, I try to exaggerate my joke to the point of being completely unbelievable, but I deliver it in a matter-of-fact fact voice that tends to make it sound credible. I will brag that I paid only ninety bucks for a five-dollar item. And when I hear, "You've got to be kidding," I know the response really means, "You'd better be kidding because otherwise you're an idiot." And my mission has succeeded.

If I follow such an assertion with a "just kidding" disclaimer, it's because there are some wily folks who, in the very pretense of buying the baloney, will flip the situation and make me the fellow limping with a pulled leg, giving them the last laugh.

An office I worked at many years ago had a copier that was prone to jamming. One young woman in particular seemed to be the one to clog it up. I watched her one day and, with great authority, corrected the way she pressed the keys. I taught her to center her index finger on the button and to push it straight and carefully, explaining that an oblique depression could cause the paper to disambiguate in its path, the mechanism to seize, and general mayhem to ensue. From my observation, she never again failed to articulate properly her contact with the keyboard, and I expect she has maintained this virtue throughout her business career. It did not stop the jams, but at least she could blame them on the insides of the machine and not sloppy human interface.

The dream of the inveterate kidder is to create a silly fiction that will take on a life of its own. For that reason, I salute the person, lost to antiquity, who invented the Easter Bunny. I was seventeen that Easter morning when Dad asked me to help him hide the eggs. Heartbroken and incredulous, I cried, "You have got to be kidding me!" Months later, I was disabused of the Santa myth as well. It was a rough year, but I have since gotten even.

To you, my reader, I make the assurance that I take my craft seriously. I would never stoop as an author to foolish exaggeration such as I might use in normal conversational discourse, so you may put your full faith and trust in every word I put to paper. I kid you not.

My Grandmother's Diary

Entry of December 28, 1943: This book was a gift from Dennis Payton Knight to his Grandmother, Mrs. Ida May Payton, for her Christmas gift on Christmas Day of 1943 when Denny was three months and twenty-one days old. On our return trip from California, we stopped off at Laramie and observed the Christmas season, arriving there on Thursday a.m. and leaving on Sunday p.m. for home after having a wonderful Christmas with Geraldine, Mickey, Jerry, Maureen, and Denny.

On that date of the first writing in her new diary, Grandma was herself the age of sixty-six years, three months, and twelve days. She lived another nineteen years, passing away in 1962 at the age of eighty-five.

For most of us, the memories of our grandmothers are treasured over the years, as are mine of Ida May Payton. We have pictures in the Knight family of Grandma dressed in her Sunday best, but the image that always comes to my mind has her in a print dress and apron. It shows her silver hair in a bun, her bespectacled eyes sparkling, and her smile, which was at its best every day of the week, not just on Sundays.

That visage has her bending from the waist before me, instructing me in the art of tying my shoes, leading me through the steps until I had succeeded, which was an achievement for both of us. It seems but a trivial, baby step memory, yet it serves me as a profound and lifelong model in the mutual arts of teaching and learning.

All my memories of Grandma are fond, yet those when I was about fifteen are also bittersweet. She had reached her eighties then and was well into what we knew as her second childhood. It was a trying time for Mom and especially for Grandpa, who had to deal with her diminishing capacity every day. It began with short-term memory lapses that became dangerous when she would lose track of a boiling pot or abandon a plugged-in iron.

I spent the summer before my junior year in Loveland with my grandparents, ostensibly to help watch after Grandma and to free Grandpa to do some fishing. As it turned out, he did not fully trust that I could handle her, or he just wanted to share the fun because he would take us both along on adventures through the countryside. The three of us would talk, laugh, and enjoy each other's company while driving over county roads or up the narrow canyon of the Big Thompson River.

That summer, she began to call me Geraldine, the name of her daughter and my mother, and concurrently speak to Grandpa about me as "our little man." She loved me to read storybooks to her as she reclaimed in her senility the joy of being a child.

I found it easy that summer to make some money doing work for elderly people in my grandparents' neighborhood. One of my regular jobs was mowing the lawn of a woman across the street who was herself in dementia, an angry form at that. She was known to lock her husband out of the house, leaving him only the shelter of their screened-in back porch. I was a bit afraid of ringing her doorbell to ask for money at the end of my work, but she always paid me without locking me up.

It was a summer of rich experience for me that my teenage psyche could have understandably resented, but from it, I gained a strong connection to my grandparents and their friends and neighbors. I am in that same demography of seniors now, but it doesn't seem foreign because I've always felt part of that world.

The medical and social understanding of dementia has seen a lot of progress, and we have learned that it has many manifestations, most commonly Alzheimer's disease. There are new treatments for sufferers and hope for their families.

I did not see my grandmother in 1958 as having a disease, but as having simply entered a new phase of life, one from which I knew she could never emerge. Our love for her was never diminished by her circumstances nor was her capacity to love or be loved.

STRAWBERRIES

The one predictable thing about the growing season on the Laramie Plains is that it will be short. The high altitude makes summers cool and pleasant, but they are bookended by deep frosts late in the spring and early in the fall.

Plains people are not easily discouraged though, even by the elements. Dirt is dirt, and twelve weeks ought to be plenty of time to raise a cucumber or tomato. Chemicals and bedding plants might make gardening in Laramie a practical venture today, but sixty years ago, you started with seed and fertilizer (the real stuff).

Despite the odds, with seven kids grazing, it made good sense for Mom and Dad to grow some of our own produce. So, along about Memorial Day, when he was sure the last spring frost was indeed the last, Dad grabbed a couple of us boys to help him turn the soil in what he optimistically called "the garden."

When the bed was plowed, raked, and ready, Mom brought out the packets of seeds: carrots, radishes, green onions, lettuce, beets, and spinach. By evening, rows were planted, each labeled with a seed envelope fastened to a stick pushed firmly into the soil. But this was Wyoming, and by morning, the winds had scattered the signage afar.

On the Fourth of July, when America's real farmers were standing in knee-high corn, our sparse garden showed but lacy hints of carrots, some stunted green onions, and a healthy row of radishes. The carrots and onions were disappearing because of jackrabbits (or a sneaky brother), so Mom pulled them early to garnish a single family salad. Ultimately, the September harvest brought us only radishes, but plenty of them. We had them at lunch and dinner for weeks, and none of us had the courage to complain.

I have now set the stage to tell you about the strawberries. Dad came home from work on the railroad one June morning and talked about how Mr. Joy, his engineer on that trip, had bragged about his strawberry patch. The fact of growing strawberries in Laramie was noteworthy indeed, but even more, the plants were shooting off runners, as they should, establishing new strawberry plants and creating a general congestion in his garden. To ease this strawberry jam, Mr. Joy suggested Dad and some of his pals might help him thin it out and they could each take some plants for themselves.

So the next morning, Dad gathered his friends, Lawrence and Oren, and off to Mr. Joy's they went. They selectively removed ninety-six plants, and Mr. Joy was pleased, inviting the men in for a belt. Well, after a general discussion of agronomy in the High Plains and then another round, the three new farmers went on over to Oren's to plant his berries, leaving Mr. Joy behind to admire his.

They placed thirty-two plants neatly in the place Oren had prepared and celebrated with another wee drop. After further discussion of Western agriculture led to debate on United States farm policy, they passed the bottle again, and then Dad took Lawrence home to plant his strawberries, leaving Oren behind to admire his.

It was a simple matter to plant thirty-two more strawberries, though neatness no longer counted, and Lawrence asked Dad in for just one more nip. They discussed the administration in Washington, Agriculture Secretary Ezra Taft Benson, and other such bull fertilizer. Lawrence poured another, and Dad decided he must get home to plant his strawberries, leaving Lawrence behind to admire his.

The sun had been up on that summer day for a good fifteen hours, but it was by the dim light of a quarter-moon that Dad finally got his runners in the ground. When the new morning brought Mom out to admire her new strawberry bed she found peeking up from the soil, the roots of thirty-two plants, properly spaced and neatly arranged, each planted upside down.

We did not have strawberries that year, and I believe our folks never again attempted to cultivate edible plants. Mom's agricultural ambitions shifted from turnips to tulips and from parsnips to petunias. Dad was happy to keep his lawn mown and watered and we lived happily ever after, as did our local green grocer.

FOOD FOR THOUGHT

Food is the subject, and it is an attractive one indeed. I have had a week to think about it, and now that I'm at my keyboard, ready to write on rutabagas and parsnips, my thoughts begin to stray to the distractions of current events and far away from the grocery department.

Why and when did it become so easy to filibuster in the Senate? Shouldn't they at least be required to read *Pilgrim's Progress*, *The Scarlet Letter*, or the dictionary?

When did it become the singular mission of the party in the minority to make the president fail, and how can that ever be good for America? And when did they scuttle the term, "the loyal opposition"?

Don't you hate the phrase, "politically correct"? It started innocently as a way to get Americans to speak respectfully to and about each other, but the cynics have co-opted it to become a pejorative against simple goodwill.

If you have made such a place for yourself in society that you live in a gated community, shouldn't your teenage son be safe enough to walk to the store and spend some of his allowance on candy and a soda?

What is it like for a mother or father, regardless of social position, to have "that talk" with a black son entering his teens, the discussion that tells a boy never to run in public and to carry nothing in his hands lest he be thought to be stealing or carrying a gun?

What cynical thing does it say about us as a society when we call a person's unquestioned and indubitable right to self-defense the "Make My Day" law? And when and why did we entrust the authority for our defense to a volunteer neighborhood watchman with a gun?

What does it say about the television pawnbroker polishing an AK-47 machine gun on camera and adoring it as "this beautiful lady"?

A headline in the *Denver Post* of Sunday, March 25, 2012, asked, "When lifers kill in prison, is it a waste to prosecute them?" On that, I guess the jury is still out.

Is it the War on Drugs that makes our prison system such an industry of growth? Private prison corporations have lobbyists in Denver pressing to maintain or strengthen sentencing guidelines to keep their industry expanding with a continuous flow of nonviolent offenders swept up in the War on Drugs.

Will the War on Drugs never end? On April 12, 2012, *Time* reported our country then had 760 prisoners per 100,000 citizens. The next highest is Brazil with 242. Japan has 93. On *The 700 Club*, televangelist Pat Robertson, that bastion of reactionary conservatism, accidentally admitted reality when he declared the War on Drugs a failure.

If we are jailing three to ten times more of our people than other civilized nations, aren't we trying to absorb back into our society three to ten times more ex-convicts than any other country? Try to put an ex-con to work anywhere, doing anything that will not send her or him back to prison.

Now, I will finally get to the topic at hand. What's for lunch?

THE INTERNATIONAL HAPPINESS OF PANCAKES

Pancakes are one of the earliest and most widespread of foods, made in prehistoric times using rocks for the grinding of available grains and hot, flat stones to cook them on. The ancient Greeks made pancakes called *tagenias*, and through the centuries, the art of making and eating pancakes has been mastered with similarities and differences in nearly every culture.

In Scotland and Ireland, pancakes are known as Scotch Pancakes, drop scones, or griddle cakes. They are known as *crempog* in Wales. In England and other parts of the United Kingdom, including Canada and Australia, they enjoy a special Pancake Day on Shrove Tuesday, the day before Ash Wednesday, as a way to use up supplies of sugar, fat, eggs, and other rich foods that are traditionally given up for Lent.

Thin, light French *crêpes* and the Italian *crespelle* are used in the cuisines of both countries as savory and sweet dishes. In Germany, pancakes are called *pfannkuchen*, meaning "pan" and "cake" or *eierkuchen* in Berlin. *Kaiserschmarm* is a light caramelized pancake filled with fruits and nuts first prepared for the Kaiser in Austria. The Dutch enjoy *pannenkoeken* and eat them for dinner with fillings of apples, cheese, ham, or bacon, as well as a molasses called *stroop*.

The list goes on. In Sweden, they are *pannkakor*, *lettu* in Finland, and *pönnukaka* in Iceland. Russians enjoy light *blintzes* and thicker *blini*. Like the Pancake Day in Great Britain, the Russians have Pancake Week to enjoy *blinis* just before the onset of Lent.

Pancakes in the African regions of Djibouti, Ethiopia, and Somalia are known as *injera*. In Ethiopia, small pieces of *injera* are torn and used as utensils to grasp stews and salads for eating.

In America, pancakes are also called hotcakes, griddle cakes, or flapjacks. The batter of eggs, flour, and milk or buttermilk and a leavening agent such as baking powder is ladled onto a hot surface and spreads to form a circle in a thickness of about a quarter of an inch. These light, fluffy delicacies are usually served at breakfast with combinations of maple syrup, butter, jam, fruits, honey, powdered sugar, whipped cream, or molasses.

American prospectors and pioneers would carry a pot of living sourdough, and it could last indefinitely, needing only flour and water to replenish it. Sourdough pancakes are now a particular specialty in Alaska.

Another uniquely American variety, the johnnycake, is a cornmeal flatbread that had its origin among the early indigenous peoples because corn is native to our continent. The johnnycake is still popular in New England and as far south as the West Indies and Bermuda.

Eat hearty.

The Nearsighted Sharpshooter

I am proud to have served my country well for my three years in the Army, but frankly, I wasn't much of a soldier. I did train and qualify as a sharpshooter and, in the doing, received a blue medal, but it isn't saying much because that is the minimum to stay in the Army, and it is far from being an expert. I qualified again every year but barely, and for that, I blame myopia, not quite corrected with Army glasses.

I was also required every year to run a mile in eight agonizing minutes. I guarantee I took the corners as tightly as I could, hoped the sergeant had a generous stopwatch, lunged across the finish line, and crawled back to the barracks.

In other words, I was no lean, mean fighting machine, but I was well suited to be where my leaders wanted me, that of being a clerk typist, and not in the infantry either. I was in what, at least in the early sixties, was probably the least military group of all, Army Aviation.

Congress had elevated the great Army Air Corps that helped win World War II to become a separate branch of service, the United States Air Force. That was not us. We flew Bird Dogs and helicopters, staying close to the troops on the battle lines, affording them reconnaissance and swift movement.

The Vietnam War rose up angrily just as I was ending my military service. It proved the importance of close air support, and I will always be proud of the contributions of my friends in Army Aviation, the pilots, and enlisted men.

I was the person who, when the outfit went into the field to practice its role in warfare, would stay back at the fort to order the parts and answer the telephone. Or as I used to tell my buddies, I was the guy they left behind to type up the surrender notice. I pondered which general and whose army I might put in the *Surrendered By* box, already knowing my outfit and my general would go in under *Surrendered To*.

Parade of Tubas, Tutus, Taiko, and Towing

When you are lucky enough to have a kid in the band, it's a cinch you will be going to parades. Thomas, my older son, focused on music at Horizon High School. He learned to play all the brass instruments, moving easily among them. He played French horn in concert bands and trombone for jazz and interchanged among trumpet, mellophone, euphonium, and tuba in marching band.

One Christmas season, Horizon marched in Denver's Parade of Lights, and for that event, Thomas joined with the tubas. To make things festive, the parade committee encouraged different sections of the bands to depart from uniform and design their own marching attire. The Horizon tuba line of eight strapping boys answered the challenge. They assembled white leotards and, with the help of some band mothers, made chiffon tutus in shades from lime green to hot pink, a different color for each musician.

It was a hit. Crowds along the route and viewers of the broadcast had a vision of eight big, masculine boys with sousaphones, pirouetting in tutus up Broadway and through the streets of downtown Denver. If I may be so bold, it was lovely, perhaps even graceful, like a scene from *Fantasia*. Footage played and replayed on television for several days. Horizon won the marching band award that year, yet it seems not to have pleased the right folks because that was also the end forever of creative cross-dressing for bands in the Parade of Lights.

Just a few years later, Thomas and his younger brother Robert were involved in *taiko*, the Japanese art of high energy drumming that has become so popular around the world. Taiko drums are massive, and playing them is much a martial art like karate or judo.

It was about 1999 when the Parade of Lights committee asked Denver Taiko to join their event, but the group was reluctant because their drums, wonderful in festivals, are not designed for parades. Undaunted, the committee promised to build a conveyance for the drums and drummers. They built a flat cart with a steel bar for two helpers to push, and it did the trick, surviving both Friday and Saturday night editions of that year's parade.

The next year, with the same cart back in service, I volunteered to push. It really did not seem too hard, and my partner and I maneuvered the cart through the staging area and into the procession precisely as choreographed. Denver Taiko was an eruption of energy, movement, and booming rhythm as we neared the announcers and television cameras. Perhaps it was my own adrenalin to blame, but I felt a snap as the iron push bar gave way, breaking off at the weld.

The parade halted for a moment and then continued on around us while we sat momentarily marooned on the pavement. Within minutes, a quick-thinking parade marshal tied two twenty-foot lengths of rope to the front corners of the float. I took the one on the left, my partner got the right, and together we towed Denver Taiko right back into the parade, although at a new position.

There were several changes in towing partners on the other corner that night, but I managed bullheadedly to hold my own from beginning to end. I did resolve, however, that, if I ever again volunteered to join a parade, it would be in a tutu.

The Back of My Book

I expect to receive offers from all the big houses in New York for my new book, and the publisher I choose will most certainly want a blurb about me for the cover. Goodness, it will be so difficult to condense my glowing life and career in just a few lines.

I must urge my editors to at once praise with moderation yet motivate the buyer to take my book straightaway to the cash register. (Parenthetically, I am certain many of my buyers will be women because the glossy cover will feature my alluring Hemingway beard.) To that end, I have drafted a letter to my prospective publisher:

> *My Dear Mr. Schuster (I just know it will be Schuster),*
> Thank you again for your enthusiasm in bringing my tome to press, and I am happy to have selected you and Simon over those big talkers at Random House. I know you are the fellows to get the book on shelves all over the country and, in due course, around the world.
> You have asked for some liner notes, and I modestly oblige. First, I have decided not to mention the Medal of Honor. I know it will soon arise, but I am happy just for having saved the lives of so many of our young soldiers, potential book buyers all, that embattled night.
> Mention only if you must my triumph at Carnegie Hall. The reality is I only handled the clarinet riffs, except of course when I took that long set on the drums when poor Krupa got the hiccups.
> I don't know if potential readers will care that I dabble in oils either. It will suffice to drop in a reference to "Sistine Chapel" and maybe depict a scaffold. For that matter, my Oscar is but a statuette, and that Pulitzer thing is not worth mentioning at all.
> Well, Mr. Schuster, I know I am asking you to

hold my thunder. Instead, to summarize the great me, I modestly suggest to you the words of Doris Day about some other fellow. Was it Clark Gable? No matter, it would have been me if I had gotten to her first.

She said, "No actor I ever performed with had such public appeal. He was as masculine as any man I've ever known and as much a little boy as a grown man could be—it was this combination that had such a devastating effect on women. But there was nothing of 'the King' about his personality. Just the opposite. Utter simplicity. Uncomplicated. A man who lived on a simple, down-to-earth scale."

Come to think of it, Schuster, maybe that should go on the front cover, along with the beard.

MUSIC MADE IN AMERICA

Body and Soul. Summertime. 'Round Midnight. My Funny Valentine. What Is This Thing Called Love? Stella by Starlight. Autumn Leaves. Star Dust. Way Down Yonder in New Orleans. In the Mood.

These songs are part of what is sometimes called the American songbook, and they are jazz standards all. Jazz was uniquely born in America, and I believe it will live forever.

Music historians will someday consider the entire body of jazz on a level with other branches of the world's library of classical music. Indeed, Gershwin's *Rhapsody in Blue* and *An American in Paris*, along with *Porgy and Bess*, are already there. What is the work of the classical composer Leonard Bernstein's *West Side Story* if it isn't classical and jazz both? Maria, I just met a girl named Maria. Let it waft through the concert hall of your mind.

I am quite overwhelmed in looking over a list of the top thousand jazz standards. Those songs I mentioned do go to the top, of course, but if you scroll down about sixty titles, you find "Tea for Two" and "Over the Rainbow." At position ninety-nine is "Smoke Gets in Your Eyes," and then come "Bye Bye Blackbird" and "April in Paris." I could go on and on, but they are all number one in my book.

Hundreds of composers have built the great American songbook. The list includes Bernstein and the Gershwins, Richard Rodgers, Lorenz Hart, Duke Ellington, Cole Porter, Johnny Mercer, and Jerome Kern. I won't even attempt a list of great performers in the genre, but I can't help but drop the names of Louis Armstrong, Ella Fitzgerald, Frank Sinatra, and Tony Bennett.

What makes a song a standard? Wikipedia defines it as a tune or song of established popularity. Another definition I read says a standard is a composition that is held in continuing esteem and commonly used as the basis of jazz arrangements or improvisations. I believe I have already accomplished a satisfactory definition. If the mere mention of a song title brings the lyrics or melody directly to your mind, it is a standard.

Jazz is a unique product of the American experience. It was born out of a mix of African and European music traditions, and its gnarly roots reach through the cities of America from New Orleans to Chicago, New York, and Miami. It is the cool jazz of the West Coast, the avant-garde music of Miles Davis, the bebop of Dizzy Gillespie, and the Latin jazz of Tito Puente.

The mere mention of any American standard like "Willow Weep for Me" or "It's Only a Paper Moon" will put a song in a heart somewhere in Paris, Istanbul, or Hong Kong. It is music truly made in America, maybe our single greatest export, and it helps puts the whole world on "The Sunny Side of the Street."

Presidential 'Dos

It is not why we remember him, of course, but the hair and beard is how we remember Abraham Lincoln, and for that, we can thank eleven year-old Grace Bedell of Westfield, New York, who wrote to the candidate just weeks before his election,

> I have got four brothers, and part of them will vote for you anyway, and if you let your whiskers grow, I will try and get the rest of them to vote for you. You would look a great deal better for your face is so thin. All the ladies like whiskers, and they would tease their husbands to vote for you, and then you would be President.

Mr. Lincoln thanked Miss Bedell and wrote, "As to the whiskers, having never worn any, do you not think people would call it a piece of silly affectation if I were to begin it now?" Lincoln did let his whiskers grow, won the election, and, I would surmise, carried the vote of the Bedell brothers in getting there.

Perhaps the finest head of hair in presidential history crowned Andrew Jackson. It was glorious beyond what mere language can describe, but that twenty in your wallet is worth a thousand words to describe the locks swirling about Old Hickory's cranium.

And if you mention the name of George Washington, his hairdo comes to mind. In his time, it was popular for a man to wear a white wig, but Washington eschewed that as aristocratic, and he instead powdered his own light brown hair to white and tied it in a queue.

In the years since President Lincoln, there have been other bearded or mustachioed leaders, but the last seventeen chief executives have all been neatly cropped and clean-shaven. I suspect the monotony is related more to image and candidate marketing than to presidential preferences.

Political cartoonists often find hair to be the essence of caricature. John F. Kennedy had a handsome face that was easy to draw, but to this day, we would recognize him in a cartoon if it showed nothing but his full locks, which he seldom covered with a hat.

A favorite of cartoonists is Bill Clinton, who is easily depicted by his mane of white. These days, they usually make him more statesmanlike, but occasionally, you still see pure lechery in a Clinton cartoon.

Mr. Clinton's two successors to the presidency, George W. Bush and Barack Obama, both have conservative hairstyles that are hard to exaggerate, so they are each often caricatured with oversized and comic ears. If a few squiggles of wavy hair are penciled in between the ears, it's Bush, and if the pate is square and tight, it's Obama.

We can only hope that President Obama will soon get a letter from some young admirer, perhaps even one of his own daughters, to let his hair grow out, start a beard, and greatly enhance his visage for the annals of history. Short of that, perhaps he should inquire about an ear job.

Uncle Tom

We did not see a lot of him because he lived several hundred miles away. He never married or had children, but I believe Uncle Tom always took quiet pride in all of his nieces and nephews as if we were his own.

Thomas Vincent Knight was born in June 1901 to a family of eleven children. It was a slightly nomadic life because his father was moved about to superintend various sections along the Denver & Rio Grande Railroad.

In his early adult years, Tom worked at the famous Sunnyside Mine at Silverton, Colorado. The family story is that he spent only one day in the mineshaft and declined ever to go down again. There seemed to be plenty of work for him at the top, and they kept him on the payroll over the years with a variety of jobs that did not require a headlamp.

Uncle Tom was happy in his solitude, enjoying good friendships at all stages and places of his life. He had the most even temperament you can imagine, never complaining about a thing. If something was not for him, he simply did not entertain it. Tom had no interest in marriage, mine shafts, or driving an automobile. He was a nonsmoker and nondrinker, so I suppose he decided he could live without those vices as well.

Tom was nearly forty when he was drafted into the Army in the Second World War. He was injured and received a small disability pension from the government for the rest of his life. He worked in the railroad shops in Denver for a short time but soon returned to Silverton where he worked again at the Sunnyside, mostly as a caretaker.

By the late fifties, he had retired to live in a Durango boardinghouse. Every morning, weather permitting, he would walk for miles upstream and down to fish the beautiful Animas River.

In about 1970, my brother Jim and I drove down to see Uncle Tom. He was delighted with our visit, taking us to see the sights of Durango and giving us his own guided tour of Mesa Verde. He was in his late sixties then but still in shape as he led us over the walking trails and up the ladders to show us the nooks and crannies of the cliff dwellings.

Tom knew the history and lore of the railroads, the towns, the tribes, and the countryside of the Four Corners region and to its east, the San Luis Valley, where he spent his final decades at the State Soldiers and Sailors Home at Monte Vista. He had a cottage there, really kind of an efficiency apartment, where he lived independently, enjoying a mix of solitude, friendships, and things to do at the center.

He was an engaging conversationalist with a grasp of current events, taking wonder at the modern developments and luxuries of the twentieth century but imbibing in few of them. He did not like to stray far from Monte Vista, but he would sometimes take excursions organized by the Veterans Center.

One of those trips brought Uncle Tom at age ninety-four to Denver to see the Colorado Rockies, Coors Field, and his first major league baseball game. He was a big Rockies fan from their inception in 1993 and reported to our family that the new stadium was just about the finest in the world.

I do not share all the virtues of Uncle Tom, but he is my model for living a deliberately simple life and making the best of it. Thomas Vincent Knight died a happy man in December 1997.

The Solstices—Marking the Extremes

At the summer solstice in Denver, most of us who are up at dawn greet a rising sun at five thirty-two and watch it set at eight thirty-one, concluding fifteen hours of official daylight. Conversely, one hundred and eighty days later at the winter solstice in December, the sun will only be up for nine hours and twenty-one minutes, a decrease of nearly six daylight hours.

If you do not like the early mornings, you should be thankful we're on daylight savings time, or our summer solstice sunrise would have been at four thirty-two. I do not complain about the early arrival of the sun because dawn is my favorite time of day, but many people keep the shades pulled to block old Sol from creeping into their bedrooms.

In comparison to places north, we do not have it so bad in Colorado at either solstice. Using sunrise and sunset tables available on the web, I charted the lengths of days at the summer and winter solstices in cities from the Arctic to the equator. In Fairbanks on June 20, the sun rose at two fifty-eight and did not set until after midnight at twelve forty-seven for twenty-one hours and forty-nine minutes of official daylight. On Christmas Day, Fairbanks will have daylight for three hours and forty-three minutes, a swing of about eighteen hours from summer to winter, three times Denver's fluctuation of six hours.

Billings to our north will see a variance of about seven hours, while Albuquerque to our south marks a difference of less than five hours. Cities near but not on the equator fluctuate about twenty minutes, while those living directly on the line have exactly twelve hours of official daylight every day and every season of the year.

The summer solstice may be mildly irritating to those who like to sleep in, but the winter solstice and dearth of light can cause some people to experience seasonal affective disorder, a depression that can lead to hopelessness, overeating, oversleeping, loss of energy, and irritability.

Alaskans in winter are particularly prone to the disorder. An

Associated Press article in 2005 chronicled one man, reporting, "Lloyd Leavitt shrugs off the subzero freeze that blankets the town of Barrow, Alaska, each winter. It is the weeks of endless night that get to him, filling him with insatiable cravings for carbohydrates, sleep, and natural light." The article quoted a 1995 study in the *American Journal of Psychiatry* showing 10 percent of Alaskans suffer from seasonal affective disorder.

That same state's long days of summer, on the other hand, are a source of economic vibrancy in the Matanuska Valley thirty miles north of Anchorage. The agricultural boom in what is better known as the Mat-Su Valley started in 1935 as a New Deal program when two hundred families reeling from the Great Depression were relocated from the Lower Forty-Eight to the fertile region in Alaska with the promise of a better life.

With an average of nineteen hours of summer daylight, Matanuska's growers, many of whom are descendants of the original colonists, are renowned for gigantic cantaloupe, carrots, turnips, and other crops.

Cabbages exceeding one hundred pounds grow in the Mat-Su Valley at Wasilla, the town where Sarah Palin grew up to be mayor before she became governor of Alaska and then a candidate for vice president of the United States.

I cannot seem to make a connection between a one hundred-pound head of cabbage and Sarah Palin, but I thought it was worth mentioning.

THE INTERNATIONAL HAPPINESS OF ICE CREAM

With the hundreds of flavors and brands of ice cream in our country, it is quite understandable that Americans claim it as our own, like hot dogs and baseball. In fact, Americans have done many happy things with ice cream, but we did not invent it.

The ancient Greeks and Romans gathered and stored snow to mix with fruits, nectars and honey, and even wine. The Arabs may have been the first to use cream as an ingredient, sweetened with sugar rather than fruit juice, and in the tenth century, ice cream was available in Damascus and other cities in the Middle East.

In the year 1295, Marco Polo returned to Italy from the Far East with riches, including a recipe that resembles sorbet, a frozen product made from fruits and not dairy products. In the 1660s, when creative Italian cooks added cream to the mixture, it became the rich gelato we know today.

Later in that century, the indulgence came to the French public when a Sicilian opened a café in Paris serving a recipe blending milk, cream, butter, and egg yolks into a custard. The French call it *glace.* Aaaah, French vanilla. It is rich and silky, and like buying a yacht, if you have to ask how many calories, you cannot afford it.

Quaker colonists from England brought the art of ice cream to the new world. The first advertisement for the product in America appeared in New York in 1777 when confectioner Philip Lenzi announced that ice cream was available "almost every day." One New York merchant kept records of George Washington spending about two hundred dollars for ice cream in 1790, and Dolly Madison served it at her husband's inauguration in 1813. Augustus Jackson, an African American confectioner who served as a chef in the White House and created many ice cream recipes, invented a superior technique for its manufacture in 1832.

In Mexico, it is *helado*, and you can find it at *La Michoacana*, a popular chain that has been selling it for more than a century. The Germans formally call it *die eiskrem*, but mostly they just ask for *das eis*. In Ghana, *fanice* can be bought from vendors on bicycles with ice chests. In Greece, favorite *pagoto* flavors include olive oil with figs and *mavrodaphne* made from a dessert wine.

The Russians love *morozhenoe*. An indulgence called a White Russian is made with vodka added to the chilling custard. The alcohol does not cook off, so it keeps its kick. They make a Black Russian, too, with cola and vodka.

Folks in China call their ice cream *pinyin*. It comes in vanilla, chocolate, strawberry, and local flavors like black sesame and red bean. Japan imports a great deal of American ice cream, but they love a green tea flavor of their own with *anko,* a sauce made of sweet red beans.

Australians and New Zealanders are among the leading consumers of ice cream in the world. Hokey Pokey is a popular flavor there and in Japan as well. It is vanilla with lumps of honeycomb. The name derives from Italian ice cream vendors in New York and London singing out words that sound like "hokey pokey" to the Anglo ear.

Ice cream has conquered the world. It is a delight for every palate, and every culture has refined it in a way that makes it uniquely theirs. In this country, we love our ice cream rich and creamy, piled with toppings, and maybe landing on a split banana, proclaiming it as American as apple pie.

UNDER THE RAINBOW

In pondering an essay on race and culture, I know there are many problems in America associated with race. The most vexing of those is the gang warfare that exists inside particular ethnic groups and races, and probably at the root of all that is economic injustice.

I am happy to reflect, however, that we do not live in a color-blind society. That is not even worthy as a goal because the concept by its very end denies the differences that imbue the human race. I have chosen to write my piece as a celebration of race and culture as I relate personal experiences of the kinds we all share, gazing with full perception of color on that marvelous rainbow we call America.

I grew up in the distinctly white world of Laramie, Wyoming, but on what was called, euphemistically, "the other side of the tracks." Our neighbors on the block were black, white, and Mexican. There were on our street tarpaper shacks and traditional houses like our own. As children, we played together, and some of the friendships we made endure yet today.

When I was in the Army as a twenty-year-old, I had just been transferred from Alaska to my second duty assignment in New Jersey when one of my fellow soldiers named Lee wandered over to my bunk, showed me a piece of paper, and asked me to check it out. It was a simple drawing looking down on two men, one white and one black, facing off with their arms forming a circle and their fists nearly touching. One of the four hands clenched a knife. I knew I was being tested, so I looked twice to be sure of what I was seeing.

When Lee returned in a few minutes, reclaimed the paper, and posed the obvious question, I answered that it was the white guy with the knife. I had passed. Later that day, we engaged in conversation and got to know each other better. Although he could have passed for white, he came from a black father and white mother. Lee was raised as a black man and associated himself within that circle. The armed forces were integrated barely a decade earlier, and blacks and whites still self-segregated in the mess hall and NCO club. Lee would sometimes invite me along when he was with others of his race. They were not all quite so ready to accept me based on a single dubious test, but I felt neither uncomfortable in their presence nor compelled to push myself on them. That was fifty years ago, and racial integration is still a work in progress.

In 1974, I married a woman whose ancestors happened to have come from Japan. She was a third-generation American, or *sansei*, whose parents and grandparents were farmers in Northeastern Colorado. Her family was through and through part of all aspects of the culture of the Western United States, yet they maintained their own wonderful Japanese traditions. Together, we had two sons, Thomas and Robert. I used to tell them they were not by halves Japanese and Irish, but all Irish, all Japanese, and all American.

As I write this paragraph thinking about my boys, my iPod happens by coincidence to be playing a piece by Denver Taiko, for which both Robert and Thomas drummed with passion. It's a reminder to me of my love for them both, how their lives were enhanced by being members of different rich cultures, and how my own life has been enhanced through them.

My little experiences are my own, but I believe millions of people all over the country share them in different ways every day. The United States is a festival of races, ethnicities, and cultures. We play the pipes of Scotland and the guitars of Spain. We dance the polkas of Germany, the waltzes of Austria, the mudras of India, and the sambas of Latin America. We thrill to the powwow drums of Native Americans, the *djembe* drums of Africa, and the *taiko* of Japan. Our own musical traditions of country music and jazz have evolved from the rhythms of Africa, the fiddles of Ireland, and the horns and woodwinds of Europe.

What a splendid rainbow.

Questions in the Carnage

For the folks who live in my seniors' community of Windsor Gardens, the Century 16 in Aurora is our neighborhood movie theater. It's the one closest to us, and with its multitude of features playing every day, it's where we often go. I doubt there were any of us there for the premiere of *The Dark Knight Rises*, but we likely have connections to some who were. It was a full house, an event for the young who have the energy for a midnight movie and a fascination for the campy but ever more violent Batman franchise. Some even wore costumes.

Shortly after midnight on Friday, July 20, 2012, a man in the theater calmly left his seat, passed through the emergency exit near the screen, propped open the door, and returned moments later, armored from head to foot, wearing a gas mask. Then, in a matter of only minutes, as time stood still, he methodically took twelve young lives, injured fifty-eight others, and fractured the peace of the world.

Journalists have told and retold us who, what, when, and where, leaving us to ponder to this day the final question, why. Was there a single triggering event in the life of the shooter that wrenched him away from years of work and study toward a promising career as a life-giving neuroscientist? Did he have a fascination with violent video games and movies that left his psyche desensitized to death, finding glamour in bloody carnage? Was it a warped sense of irony that brought him to dramatically seize the stage to play the diabolical antihero of the Batman series, the Joker, just as gunfire erupted on the screen? Had he quietly waited for that cue to begin his reign of terror?

The question of why the massacre happened will be answered, we hope, through the painstaking process of a public trial. In that regard, we are fortunate because the coward, unlike so many depraved killers before him, spared his own life at the end of his siege.

But another why needs to be answered. The killer purchased all his guns and ammunition quite legally, leaving us to wonder why it should be legal for any civilian who is not part of the law enforcement community to have access to an assault weapon or the magazines that give those weapons their terrible rapid firepower.

Assault weapons, banned until 2004, became legal again simply because profiteering gun makers hold our democratic society, ironically, at gunpoint. Congress and state legislators kowtow to the industry and its lobbying puppet, the National Rifle Association, and woe to any presidential candidate who makes even oblique reference to managing assault weapons.

The NRA has campaigned for decades under a half-truth, "Guns don't kill people; people kill people." The full truth is that people with guns kill people. Tragic events move us to tears, reflection, prayer, and words, but they haven't carried us to action.

Maybe this time.

The Silver Dollar Tossel

This piece is a fun collaboration with my niece Cameron Clay, which we wrote in 2012 when Cameron was about thirteen.

The brisk air nipped at Claire's fingers. Her rhythmic execution of "Silver Bells" captivated holiday shoppers allergic to department stores. Claire was accustomed to crowds gathering when she tickled the keys on one of the many brightly painted pianos happily placed in the outdoor elements along Denver's Sixteenth Street Mall. Pedestrians would stop to listen, and leave coins or folding money in the tin cup she placed on the piano top.

It had been a good day, and when she counted her proceeds that evening, reserving cash for food and the rent for her Colfax efficiency, she came across a shiny silver dollar in the bottom of the tin cup. She left it there because it seemed symbolically wrong to spend that treasure in her struggle to make ends meet.

The seasons moved on, and so did Claire. Her work as a busker led to a gig at Denver's Dazzle jazz club and, with that, a regular paycheck along with some fame. The tin cup was relegated to her kitchen cabinet, but the silver dollar stayed right there in the bottom.

Claire was still living in the efficiency and using a coin laundry down the street. Being a child of frugality, she would worry over the enigma of discarding dryer lint, lovely and fresh with the scent of Downy. One afternoon, she nonchalantly dropped the fluffy clump in the pocket of her wet raincoat along with snips and snails and odd things she had come across, like that strange seed in the shape of an almond, ready to sprout.

As the coat hung overnight on a hook in her apartment, something peculiar happened. From the pocket emerged a single leafy stem, maybe thirty inches long, bearing a fruit Claire had never seen before. It was about the size of an orange but with a smooth, caramel skin. She took a bite. It had the taste of her grandma's English toffee, right down to the crisp, sweet, coffee-colored flesh with another almond like seed in the middle. It was delicious, and it made her feel like she had eaten a full meal. Her appetite remained satisfied all day, and she had yet another seed to show for it.

She tossed that seed in the pocket with lint and other stuff, and in the morning, another stem emerged, bearing the same fruit, just as filling and delicious. This went on daily for the rest of the week, and Claire was always full, spending not a dime on groceries.

Finally, one morning she became curious and emptied the pocket on the table. She discovered her mystery plants had actually been taking root in the dryer lint still smelling like Downey.

She looked for something in the kitchen to toss her lint and seeds in, but that tin cup with the silver dollar was not quite large enough. So she put on the coat, took the silver dollar off to the dollar store, and invested in the finest pot a silver dollar could buy, one nice enough to be that one special thing she had been saving her dollar for.

She filled the new pot with the old dryer lint, and it became the growing medium for a harvest of one delicious fruit per day. Because it involved the act of tossing a seed in the lint, she began calling the lovely fruit a "tossel."

Claire got enough nourishment from her tossels, and she could skip eating them on Tuesdays to build an inventory of the seeds. She went to laundries all over Capitol Hill, collecting Downy-scented lint. She bought the dollar store out of pots, rented a garage where she started a small growing operation, moved it to a farm when it got too large, and then bought more farms. Eventually, thanks to Claire's discovery of the reaction of a seed with laundry lint, the tossel ended world hunger, and that silver dollar had been a big part of it.

Claire is now a billionaire, but a dilemma plagues her. The Center for Disease Control has declared an epidemic that has the world wheezing, sneezing, and scratching. To do the right thing, she must now spend her fortune, maybe all of it, to find something that will give relief to the victims of that dreaded new allergy called tosselitis.

Dad's Canary

Dad liked birds. He would awaken to their songs, and then, as he sipped his morning coffee, he would watch their playful activities at the feeders he kept filled along with fresh water daily in the birdbath.

And so it was no surprise to us when Dad brought home the yellow canary. He bought it for its music, but its first day in residence yielded only silence. After all, the canary was but hours removed from the dime store, the cage and environment was new, and hovering all around was a family of overly eager humans anticipating his first solo. Who could sing under those conditions?

After the second and third day without birdsong, Dad began actively coaching. He sat beside the cage and whistled until his throat constricted and his repertoire ran out. Then he played his albums of Viennese waltzes in hopes of inspiring his feathered companion with the classics. By day five, it was pathetic disillusionment. The bird was obviously defective, typical dime store junk. Wherever the hell they got their birds, it was not the Canary Islands.

But despair not. Dad rose as a phoenix inspired and flew to the record store where he found, against all reasonable hope, right there in Laramie, a phonograph record of singing canaries. It surely cost more than the bird, but at this point, who could care? Dad bought the record, put it on the Zenith, adjusted the volume, and sat back. One can only ponder what bird messages were coming out, but based on the way the canary came to life, I'd venture they were mostly mating calls. From the opening stanza, our canary expanded his chest and delivered responsive sonatas, validating his reason for being and, finally, Dad's investment.

As long as the record played, the bird sang with his melodies wafting sonorously through the neighborhood. Birds of all feather flew in and, given our dog's vertical leap, perched as close as they dared. We even saw a hawk circling over the house, and if not for the brass cage, it might have swooped in for a lemon dessert.

When the phonograph was quiet, however, so too was the bird.

He just needed something yellow to sing with, and he could thus be activated or stilled with the press of a switch on the Zenith.

Fame is fleeting even for a songbird, and as weeks passed, the canary was turned on with diminishing frequency. By fall, its singing career waned, and he served mostly as a newspaper critic, if you get my drift.

To Mom was left the monotony of feeding and cage maintenance, and we will now consider the evidence that she may have thought less of the bird than did Dad and her seven kids. Always a modern woman, she used the most effective products available in the fifties.

Today, we can buy a bazooka more easily than we can get a can of bug spray with the power she used that day, but she always maintained she was only controlling flies. Her words declared innocence, but her eyes belied her when she told the story of spraying the house, going to the grocery, and returning to find Dad's bird at the bottom of the cage, legs up, stiff as a board. I believe the canary would still be around to this day if he had taken to doing something useful, such as catching flies.

PUT THAT IN YOUR PIPE

I am challenged to write on the subject of humor. Now, I am a man who fancies himself a humorist, and I can tell you that it's easier to write humorously about anything than it is to write intelligently about the singular abstraction of humor. Love and hate are funny contradictions, as are their frequently changing dance partners, peace and war. Politics, pomposity, pathos, pulchritude, and horses in bars are fodder. All these things and more I can write about and even give you a chuckle or two.

But what the devil is this thing we call humor? In the manner of modern scholars, I have been poking at it all week, and it seems to defy simple science. All I can relate to you is what some savvier people have had to say.

Aristotle said, "Humor is the only test of gravity, and gravity of humor; for a subject which will not bear raillery is suspicious, and a jest which will not bear serious examination is false wit."

Mark Twain said, "Humor must not professedly teach and it must not professedly preach, but it must do both if it would live forever." He also said, "Humor is the great thing, the saving thing. The minute it crops up, all our irritations and resentments slip away and a sunny spirit takes their place."

Erma Bombeck said, "Humor is a spontaneous, wonderful bit of an outburst that just comes. It's unbridled, it's unplanned, it's full of surprises."

My single favorite author and humorist, James Thurber, told Edward R. Murrow in a television interview, "The wit makes fun of other persons; the satirist makes fun of the world; the humorist makes fun of himself."

In his 1964 autobiography, Charlie Chaplin claimed, "All I need to make a comedy is a park, a policeman and a pretty girl." Horace Walpole asserted, "The world is a tragedy to those who feel, but a comedy to those who think." Hugh Elliot stated, "If there's one thing I know, its God does love a good joke."

Larry Gelbart of *M*A*S*H* fame said, "One doesn't have a sense of humor. It has you." Mel Brooks said, "Tragedy is when I cut my finger. Comedy is when you walk into an open sewer and die." In a more thoughtful moment, Brooks said, "Humor is just another defense against the universe."

Peter Ustinov said, "Comedy is simply a funny way of being serious." Ralph Waldo Emerson said, "Wit makes its own welcome, and levels all distinctions. No dignity, no learning, no force of character, can make any stand against good wit."

On the daunting task at hand, E. B. White told us, "Humor can be dissected as a frog can, but the thing dies in the process and the innards are discouraging to any but the pure scientific mind." Robert Benchley cinched it and clinched it by saying, "Defining and analyzing humor is a pastime of humorless people."

Put that in your pipe and smoke it.

The Nattering Gnat

I have challenged the writers in my circle to unshackle their wits and write pure, simple nonsense. As I begin applying my own imagination to the task, however, I realize the difficulty of it. Interlopers like Lewis Carroll and J. K. Rowling have already used up all the good nonsense available. They have squandered it on trivialities like *Alice in Wonderland* and *Harry Potter.*

Sure, there was a time when the idea of a Flash Gordon shooting through space seemed to be nonsense, but since then, humans have walked on the moon and armed themselves with lasers. The crazy nonsense of Dick Tracy's two-way wrist radio has become real now, in the form of a combination global positioning device, personal assistant, telephone, and movie camera. And while we still hear nonsense every day about big, hairy monsters who sasquatch Washington State, I'm pretty sure someone will actually capture one soon and parade her down Main Street, and she too will have fallen from our inventory of nonsense.

I was sitting on my lanai last night, weighing the unlikely challenge of ever finding nonsense in the twenty-first century when I brushed aside a gnat. He was an annoying bugger, and I had to snatch him out of his seventeenth orbit around my cranium. Being a bit deaf these days to higher frequencies, I wouldn't even have heard him had he spoken in a voice consistent with his size, but it was a bellowing "Watch it, buddy!" that tickled my palm and triggered my fist to open and return him to his infernal orbit.

"Can't you see I'm busy?" I asked.

"I'm the only one that's busy here, Mac. You don't seem to be doing much of anything sitting there."

"I happen to be concentrating, you stupid bug. I'm on a project."

"Oh, I can see that, buddy boy. You have been oozing thought balloons for the last forty-seven minutes. They are floating all around the neighborhood congesting our flight patterns, and they're all empty. I've been sent to investigate."

"Okay, then you try it, gnat. Think me up some utter nonsense to write about, something totally impossible."

He returned to flight, somewhat irregular now, and I could hear a cough as he buzzed past my right ear, the good one. He sputtered some more, and his orbit became jerkier. I thought I could see tiny thought balloons in his wake, but let's face it, that would be ridiculous. He was a gnat.

Finally, he came in for a landing on the back of my hand and looked up at me. "Okay, buddy boy, you have me at a disadvantage. Truth is, I was hatched in an old volume of logic, physical and metaphysical. It was heavy stuff, and on my way out, I consumed every word. With that, I can tell you with no doubt in my mind that everything that is, was, or may ever be makes sense. Period. End of argument.

"The very idea of finding nonsense in this rational universe, my friend, is quite nonsensical. Now I must buzz off, buddy boy. They're sending me to the political conventions down South to check out more of those empty thought balloons. What a bunch of nonsense."

A Letter to My Tattoo Artist

Leonardo the Tattooist
Denver, Colorado

My Dear Mr. da Vinci:

 I find in the yellow pages that your studio seems to have survived the latest urban renewal on South Broadway, and I hope this letter finds you thriving and still at your art. Do you remember sweet Monica? It has been decades since you rendered her lovely, curvaceous figure on the mass of my muscular right arm.

 What a dish. She would come alive with the merest flex of my bicep, and the mates down at the pub would crowd in to watch her dance as I raised the occasional mug. Pints, all on the boys, would array before Monica and me as they cheered her oscillations. You gave her a haunting Mona Lisa smile with delicate and artistic inking, but she had an appeal even more compelling. She could really shake that thing. So could I, but that was then.

 I write today not just to see if you are still living and still tattooing, but to ask your clinical advice on certain matters concerning my Monica. It seems neither of us is aging so well. My bicep flexes neither so often, nor so dramatically, and the pretty lady has become a bit flabby. In fact, she is fat.

 Yes, she is still shaking her thing, but it is more like a tidal wave and then only when I heft a glass of water to get my daily meds down. I suppose, with some exercise of my own, she would tighten up here and there, but I fear Monica and I will never again draw the crowds and admiration of our youth.

 It is time to return her to you, her creator, to be renewed. She needs more than a facelift, Mr. da Vinci. She needs a metamorphosis. In that vein, how about making her into a butterfly? She already has achieved much of the shape. I envision adding antennae, and with a few symmetrical patterns inked into her flabbiest parts, she would take wing and flutter again. For that matter, maybe you could make her into a frog on a lily pad. It would take some filling in, but she wouldn't need the antennae. In general, in considering new incarnations for Monica, you need to be thinking broadly, very broadly. Tugboats and tubby tunas come to mind.

I have always admired Disney's dancing hippos. You could achieve that lovely effect, of course, by inking in a tutu. The challenge will be in stretching her Mona Lisa smile into the broad, toothy grin of a hippopotamus. Could you manage that and still leave it fetching?

I am hoping you will have suggestions of your own, but of course, you will first need to see us both, Monica and me. We will be downtown next week, so please get back to me soon and let me know if you feel up to the task.

By the way, da Vinci, if you are able to bring Monica back to glory, we will then need to talk about that discreet red star you once engraved on my rear end. It has gotten as big as a Texaco sign.

IT STARTED AT THE TOWER OF BABEL

> *And so God scattered them upon the face of the Earth, and confused their languages, and they left off building the city, which was called Babel "because God there confounded the language of all the Earth" (Gen. 11:5–8).*

So how many languages are there in the world? According to a report of the Linguistic Society of America in 2010, there is no scientific count, but it's in the thousands. It tells us that parts of the Bible have been translated to over twenty-five hundred languages, and so it appears the language of the earth has indeed been confounded.

I spent some time recently playing with two online translator programs, Babel Fish and Microsoft's Bing translator. I typed in quotations from Shakespeare and Twain to see how they would translate from English to French and back to English, repeating the same process with other primary languages. The programs worked quite well, which was disappointing because I was counting on getting some returns that would make an entertaining piece.

So I upped the ante to see how popular quotations would come out if translated through a succession of multiple languages. For instance, Mark Twain once wrote, "Clothes make the man. Naked people have little or no influence in society." Thirty-five translations later, it comes back in English as, "The man wore a small amount of the nude in a public place."

That was promising, so I gave the digital word grinders a larger challenge, some lines from my piece, "My Career as a Male Belly Dancer." Here is what I originally wrote:

> It was a grand opportunity to display my unique and only performance talent. I could roll my stomach in a contraction and expansion of belly muscle that began at the sternum and proceeded in rolling waves to and from my waist. Nobody outside my family had ever seen me do this, and I was excited and not

even a bit embarrassed to bring it to the public. Ray Walston could do it, too, but I was better.

I visited Woolworths and a grocery store to buy some colorful cotton yardage to pin around my waist, some cotton cord, and a nice, round coconut. With materials in hand, limited knowledge of coconuts, and absolutely no experience with brassieres, I proceeded.

Eight translations later, my lines bounced back to me in English confounded:

It is a good opportunity to bring my talent into view, and the only secret is really my only talent agents. This day is in my stomach will start narrowing and broadening of the sternum in the abdominal muscles and continue to swing back, and my family, I saw it and it is not even the public is excited, a bit embarrassed. Ray Ray Walston.

I visited the Volvo and hangs around the waist and a large supermarket in cotton, circular cable, some coconut. Promotional material in your hand and coconut bras and absolutely no experience, he said. Using tools can dig a hole, cut half a coconut, my father arranges it. Also discovered a difficult technical problem. Maidenform gravitational problems, even when I load my people resolve or coconut and light enough and some neck depends on the color of the pen do I poke a knife-tip. Breast cancer well, connect the power of steam. And my mother lent me double cheek rouge.

I ran the piece through another twenty-seven translations, and the confounded was compounded, right to the end where the double cheek rouge was now "shown in red color vampire courts."

I hope I will someday write a book with a worldwide demand, but I fear that, when it happens, I am going to have to hope my publisher uses something other than Bing to get it ready for the Polish market, or my cheeks will be definitely be in the red color of vampire courts.

STORYTELLERS, ONCE UPON A TIME

There may be several things that we think distinguish humans from the animals, but one certainly is the ability to tell stories. It is how we, as families and societies, pass on history, knowledge, and lore, and it must have begun right along with the development of words.

Storytelling blossomed in the millennia before the invention of letters and literacy. It is how some of our great works came to us, epics like *A Thousand and One Arabian Nights* which collected the ancient stories of Persia and Arabia. The historic English story of *Beowulf* is merely the writing down of an old heroic poem set in Scandinavia. The use of poetry, rhythm, and song allow storytellers the world over to commit to memory and pass their heroic tales along, word for word, to the next generations of storytellers.

Homer is credited for bringing us those graceful epics of ancient Greece, *The Iliad* and *The Odyssey*, but in doing so, he drew from the deep well of tales handed down by storytellers in the centuries before him.

In pre-Christian Ireland, the *seanchai* spoke wondrously of banshees, fairies, leprechauns, and the dreaded, shape-changing *pooka*. If their fancies now seem pure blarney, recall the Sirens and Cyclops of the *Odyssey* before you raise your protest. Modern bards continue to ply the Emerald Isle, competing for awards at events like the Mummers Festival in Galway.

The written word expanded our ability to memorialize and explain history and ideas, but it hasn't stopped the rich tradition of oral storytelling. In Africa, the least literate continent of the Earth, the art of the elders continues to thrive in profound ways. The Swahili people on the coast of Kenya pass down moving poetry, some of which has been influenced by Islam with stories of genies. Other ethnic groups have stores of riddles, proverbs, and sayings that are an important aspect of everyday speech.

The Kikuyu, also in Kenya, sing elaborate poems and riddles learned by heart, rhythmically accompanied by a decorated gourd.

Many pieces, called *gicandi*, are very long and often consist of over a hundred stanzas. Oral literature is taught and preserved in the modern education system of Kenya, and it includes a requirement for students to collect folklore from their parents and grandparents. They believe it to be an important part of their heritage and are taking steps to preserve it.

The Native American culture is known for passing its history from generation to generation over centuries without written languages. All the tribes had revered storytellers, men and women, to teach their history, customs, rituals, and legends through vivid narratives. As in other parts of the world, these storytellers are still actively engaged in preserving their cultures.

Before I close this piece, I want to mention the importance of storytellers in the collection of family lore and histories. The Knight kids learned to watch for the shine in Dad's Irish eyes as he was about to embark on a story or two of our forebears. We would listen to wondrous tales like that of how our family name lost its "Mc" when a great or great-great grandfather, then named McKnight, was caught rustling cattle and given the choice of giving up his Mc or hanging. His choice preserved the family line, and I thank the heavens for that. Along with it, Dad inherited his twinkle and passed it on to me.

I hope you have some twinkling eyes in your family, too.

My Time in the Arena

It was a sunny afternoon in Denver when I arrived at the time and place of battle, having trained for weeks in a combination of exercises that featured spins, bursts, and thrusts. The arriving gladiators were old and young, female and male, plain and pretty, strange and common; all foes to be reckoned with.

We could see, hear, and smell the ozone of electricity emanating from the arena. Our mounts waited on the stadium floor, each soon to be claimed by one of us in a promise of spoils to the quickest, an asset I was sure my training had honed.

We vied for position at the entrance, and the arena master finally threw open the gate. I tore swiftly for the vessel I had picked, a sleek silver number that seemed already well positioned and ready for a worthy captain like me. In fact, I had been so intent on driving Silver Streak that I was unprepared to make another choice when I arrived to find a female combatant in a yellow dress already inserting herself a little indelicately, I might add, behind my wheel.

With my claim having been so rudely commandeered, I surveyed the field and found only one unattached vessel, a faded blue job jammed in a corner. Old Blue might not have been my first preference, but I leapt in anyway and readied myself for the contest.

As we waited the start, I stubbornly held in view the girl in the yellow dress gripping the wheel of Silver Streak, her mean, green eyes running a pantheon of fiery expressions. She did not seem to notice me, but I was determined she soon would.

The arena boss rang a bell and tossed a lever, and the game was on. Movement on the circuit, pursuant to American racing tradition, was counterclockwise but haphazardly so with aggressive charges, deft evasions, and blunt collisions. The atmosphere sizzled. It was alive in shrieks, laughter, and whiplash. I was knocked off my moorings several times, but I gave as good as I got.

I kept Silver Streak and the yellow dress in my vengeful sights, but she seemed always a lane out of reach, so I tried to rattle her from afar with chain collisions that never quite got through. I lost track of her in yet another cycle of bumping and being bumped around the circuit when a massive impact in my blind spot at Blue's left rear bumper, stunned me. We went into a spin and I caught glimpses of mean, green eyes sparkling in triumph.

The arena master and lord of our universe then summarily and without determination of a clear victor reversed the lever to end the hostilities. I separated myself sadly from Old Blue. As I walked unsteadily to the exit of that wonderful old bumper car ride at Elitch Gardens, the girl ahead of me in the yellow dress looked back, fluttered her big green eyes and smiled. I knew it was only for me. I may have lost the battle, but my spirits won the war.

Old Dogs, New Tricks

Just about every outfit in the Army has a guy they call "Pappy." It's a term of respect. Master Sergeant Daryl "Pappy" Kreutzer was in his twenty-seventh year in the Infantry, but he was only forty-seven. If the Pappy moniker was premature, so was the graying of his military buzz cut and the creased leather of his face.

Sergeant Kreutzer was busted twice in his first, hell-bent decade in the service, but his advancement since then had been steady and solid. He had seen more than his share of combat, and now he was back to his favorite duty, drilling raw recruits. He was, in his present assignment, the highest-ranking enlisted man in the outfit, and had eight subordinate drill instructors barking at anything that moved.

Like all drill sergeants before him, he used the strongest language to exorcise the namby-pamby from his young soldiers. The words were base, to be sure, but with Pappy in charge, the troops experienced them in the most artful combinations imaginable.

Also in every military unit, besides a guy like Pappy, who has actually earned the nickname, there is what they call "the Old Man," the commanding officer. The new Old Man of this company was maybe twenty-eight. His career so far had been at a desk job in Washington, and he had been given this command at old Fort Cussin to get some field experience. At least that was what Pappy surmised, but it wasn't his job to vet the man's credentials.

Picture the scene the morning Kreutzer called his sergeants in for a parlay and the pulsing anger in his face as he unwadded a single sheet of paper. "Men, you ain't going to like this, but we got ourselves a new order. What the Old Man says is, starting today, we have to clean up our damn language. We've got to address the troops without half the damned words in our damned vocabulary. In fact, I already screwed up and disobeyed this damned order three damned times. Make that four. Dammit all to hell."

Pappy kicked a chair up to the table. "All right, men, what we gotta do now is think up some brand-new cuss words. Now the beauty of them words we been using is they is versatile. They fit every situation, and there ain't nobody nowhere that don't know what they mean. That's the kind of words we've got to get. Now you boys got any ideas?"

Kreutzer's review of the order had them all dumbfounded. The old dogs of the outfit faced the challenge of creating, learning, and implementing an entirely new vocabulary of swearing or run the risk of sending soldiers off to battle without proper oral burnishing. It was a damned mess. Better make that a crying mess.

Sergeant Kreutzer called down to the mess hall for a fresh pot of coffee and the team spent hours creating and polishing up a list of brand-new cuss words. They eventually emerged with *dangt, florg, azule, balt, zummit, bushdob, quosk, moskag, noffle,* and *jakfick*. Each could be matched with common prefixes and suffixes to expand their utility and could be randomly combined for even greater effect.

They had ten glorious new words to cuss and motivate the troops, and they would not need to define one *bushdob* one. That would all be taken care of in context. No soldier would need or even dare request clarification when ordered, "*Zummit*, Jones, get yo' haid out of yo' *florg*."

Master Sergeant Pappy Kreutzer, having successfully pulled his team through the rough battle of inventing words to supersede a thousand years of perfectly good cussing, declared it a done *moskag* deal and wrapped up the *bushbob* confab by ordering his sergeants to take the troops out on a *florging* five-mile march to loosen up their *balt dangt bushbob noffles*.

"All right, men, back to work. Right now, I'm going to sign off on this *bushdob* order, take it back to the Old Man, and *jakfick* it right up his *zummit* inbox. Dammit all to hell."

The Twelve Days of Christmas, Plus One

In a quiet downtown bar on a winter's day, I came across a journal left behind on the bench at a corner booth. It doesn't have a name on it, but the writings show a feminine hand. I read the diary and came to understand why she bookmarked the page with a tear-stained bar napkin after making her last entry, set it down, and walked away. I will share some excerpts.

December 25

This is our first Christmas in a lifetime of holidays to come. It was a lovely morning with scads of nice things under the tree, but I treasure most this journal from my true love to record the days of our lives together. Then another surprise came this afternoon when the floral delivery brought a lovely partridge tethered in a pear tree. There was no sender's card, but true love blushed and grinned. I gave the silly galoot a nice big hug.

December 26

Well, I guess Christmas is not over because today true love sent another partridge in a pear tree, and this time it came with a pair of turtledoves, cooing ever so prettily. How appropriate. I hugged him again. I was terribly sad this evening when the taxi whisked him off to DIA, but I know I should be happy with what he brings in as a daring soldier of fortune. I do worry and wonder where he may be going. It is very secret, but he promises to text me every day.

December 28

Either true love is obsessed with birds, or he thinks I am. Today, there came four birds of yet a different kind, all calling incessantly, as well as three more French chickens, two more doves, and another damned partridge stuck in a damned pear tree.

December 29

Finally, something came that I can handle, a beautiful box of five golden rings. Very nice. But after today's other deliveries, I now have in my cellar five partridges, five pear trees, eight turtle doves, nine fancy chickens, and eight calling birds.

January 1

This is getting old. Today, I answered the bell to find at my door eight bowlegged broads with rubber gloves, each carrying a stool. Now what the hell do I do with them?

Over the next several entries, our journalist tallies by the day her burgeoning populations of birds and humans. The pages begin to show smudges, and nasty comments emerge about geese and swans, which are clearly messier than doves and partridges.

January 5

It is the twelfth day of the siege, and this better be the end of it because, after today's deliveries, I now have in the basement a cacophony of drummers drumming, pipers piping, swans trumpeting, geese honking, and calling birds calling. And it stinks.

January 6

Today is the Feast of the Epiphany, and I had one. The first thing I did was to meet with Pierre down at the French Café. I gave him outright the dozen partridges, twenty-two doves, thirty French hens, three dozen calling birds, forty-two geese, and forty-two swans. They will be on the menu starting tomorrow. Pierre hired the forty maids-a-milking. He will use them as cooks, servers, cashiers, bird handlers, and shift managers.

I amassed my other humans on the lawn of the courthouse and lined them up in the order of twenty pipers, thirty-six ladies, forty lords, and twelve drummers. I taught some peppy songs to my pipers, told the ladies to dance their prettiest, challenged the lords to leap their highest, helped the drummers find a beat, and sent the whole lot off on a parade down Broadway, a very long parade.

I took my forty rings to the cash-for-your-gold store, stashed the wad in my purse, went back to the courthouse, and filed for divorce.

MONEY AND MIGHT

Money buys subsistence, and a bit extra buys a better life. It represents the fruits of our own labor or sometimes that of our ancestors. It is widely but unevenly distributed, sometimes by merit, mostly by whim.

It is squandered often, but mostly it is exchanged for goods and services to sustain us and grow our families. We share with others according to our ability and heart, donate to causes we believe in, give to our institutions of worship, support our schools and government, and try to save some for a rainy day. Few of us think we ever have enough of it.

We often hear that money is the root of all evil, but something important is left out when that sentiment is expressed in its most common form. The exact phrase is in the Bible, in a letter from Saint Paul to Saint Timothy, at Timothy 6:10. "For the desire of money is the root of all evils."

I wanted to understand the quotation in full context, and in looking it up, the depth of the message took me aback.

> For we brought nothing into this world: and certainly we can carry nothing out. But having food and wherewith to be covered, with these we are content. For they that will become rich fall into temptation and into the snare of the devil and into many unprofitable and hurtful desires, which drown men into destruction and perdition. For the desire of money is the root of all evils; which some coveting have erred from the faith and have entangled themselves in many sorrows.

This reading suggests there is a transcendent point when the dollar becomes almighty and the acquisition and preservation of money becomes the very meaning and centerpiece of a life.

Those sinners populate the prisons and country clubs of

America, and if those in the former have met their due in this life, then Saint Paul has promised perdition to those who became rich in the snare of the devil. There is simple justice in that, and I could end my piece right here.

A larger evil is rooted in the desire of money that directly affects our republic. It is in how the concentrated power of the filthy rich can corrupt a democracy. It is the manipulation of a government by the wealthy for the preservation and growth of their lucre and little more.

Over time, that power has been leveraged to cram a high court with judges who ascribe freedom of speech to inhuman corporate entities to be used and abused indiscriminately and then uphold that travesty as vigorously as it would defend the rights of a single student jailed for protesting a war that makes the rich richer.

The unbridled power of wealth associates itself with a cadre of political clowns who mock the idea of equity in taxation as a redistribution of wealth, and it has steered our government into gridlock to selfishly secure the status quo.

It may not happen in my lifetime, but I believe—and I think St. Paul would agree—that the day will come when the idea of a trickle-down economy finally gives way to a system of trickle up and the filthy rich will finally be taking a bath.

The Winter Solstice or Happy New Year

The winter solstice occurs annually on December 21 or 22. In the Northern Hemisphere, it is the time at which the sun is at its southernmost point in the sky, creating the shortest day and longest night of the year. By my personal logic, it should mark the beginning of the New Year, although our Gregorian calendar fixes that about ten days later on January 1. My theory gets no support from the astronomical community that fixes the solar year as beginning at the vernal equinox, about March 21.

The Catholic Church fixed the date of January 1 to start the new calendar year to occur seven days after the anniversary of the birth of Christ and to mark the date of His circumcision as a holy day of obligation. The date of the Nativity was not settled until the year 433 when it was finally fixed on the Julian calendar as December 25, corresponding to the date then thought to be the winter solstice.

In 1582, Pope Gregory XII adopted the Gregorian calendar, which we use today. By that time, the solstice was known to occur several days earlier, about December 21, but the Pope maintained December 25 as Christmas and thereby separated that important Christian holiday from the solstice.

That separation of Christmas from the solar event was important to Christians because of the bacchanalian ways in which the early Greeks and Romans observed the winter solstice. The ancient calendar consisted of twelve thirty-day months, or three hundred and sixty days, and a five-day bonus period called Saturnalia to finish out the solar year. Because those days were outside of time, the ancients found license to behave without restriction in them, enjoying excesses of food, wine, and sexual exploits.

The solstice in today's cultures and religions represents birth and rebirth marking a new beginning and the reversal of the month-long trend to shorter days, all fodder for me to stubbornly hold to my initial declaration that it marks the year's new beginning. It is a moment for cultures around the hemisphere to celebrate the joy and optimism that the New Year brings.

The Zuni and Hopi tribes of North America celebrate Soyal on December 21 to bring the sun back from its long winter slumber and to mark the beginning of another cycle of the Wheel of the Year. It is a time for purification, using prayer sticks made prior to the ceremony to bless all the community and their homes, animals, and plants.

Of all the midwinter celebrations, Christmas, even though it is not tied to the solstice, is the most globally recognized, and it involves feasting, singing, gifts, good deeds, prayer, religious ceremony, and commercial exploitation. It, too, is really about joy and optimism.

The Germanic people first celebrated the Yule, a winter festival, as a pagan religious carnival, but it was later absorbed into and equated with Christmas. Yule is used in English-speaking countries as well to refer to Christmas, and it has led to customs enjoyed around the world such as the Yule log and Yule singing.

Mummer's Day originated in Cornwall to celebrate the solstice by dancing in disguise with blackened faces or wearing masks. Philadelphians celebrate it in the United States with a Mummers Parade, thought to be the oldest folk festival in the country.

Perhaps because their long winter nights are even more pronounced, cultures in Arctic regions acknowledge the transitional event of the solstice with symbolic events. On Saint Lucy's Day in Scandinavia, a young girl chosen to portray Lucia wears a crown or wreath with candles, a white robe, and red sash to chase away winter and bring back the sun. The Saami, indigenous peoples of Finland, Sweden, and Norway celebrate the Beiwe festival to honor the sun goddess who flies through the sky in a structure of reindeer bones.

The winter solstice is celebrated in every continent in some way by nearly every culture, and it is always an occasion of hope and a great spiritual lift to those of us who find ourselves deep in winter's doldrums. Happy New Year.

The Last Thing on Her List

Mom always had several lists going. There would be a running grocery list, of course, but she had others for the holidays and all her projects. At night, she would lie awake making lists in her mind to jot down when she arose. It was how she managed to get so much stuff done, and she loved the process.

Dad tended to spontaneity and often announced the family was leaving the next day for faraway places, or maybe he would sweep Mom off for a night of dancing in Denver. Whatever the moment, Mom would put together a list and check it off in what seemed like minutes. Dad's impulsiveness was a challenge she lived for.

As the daughter of a Methodist preacher and his wife serving in various communities in Eastern Colorado, Geraldine had come to enjoy the large Catholic farming families of those prairies and towns and dreamed of someday having many children herself. I don't think we ever heard her say that she had made a grand plan for her life, but after graduating from college, she found work at a nursery for the babies of migrant workers in Alamosa. It was there she had a blind date with Mickey Knight, the eleventh and youngest in a family of railroaders. The spontaneous Irishman proposed at the dance that same night, and they were married soon after. Was it all according to plan? Probably.

The young family grew to two children, struggled out of the Depression, and moved to Laramie. Dad found a lifetime of employment on the Union Pacific Railroad, and they resumed growing their family.

Planning not only served her well in running her household with efficiency, but it gave her time to lead our Catholic school's parent-teacher group. She was president of the Altar Society and planned the beautiful send-off when our elderly parish priest died. Mom's volunteer work with the county Democratic committee was just the job for a list maker. On the side, she sold real estate and worked in a retail store to build credits for Social Security.

Dad passed away on June 8, 1987, and Mom thrived for seventeen more years, regularly making and executing plans of all sorts. After my sister, Maureen and her husband had been transferred to Las Vegas, Mom and my other sister Kathi, who was divorced by then, decided to band together and move to Vegas as well. What with realtors and movers, you can imagine the reams of lists that she created in managing that upheaval. A few years later, Kathi remarried, and Mom went to live with Maureen.

In the spring of 2004, to celebrate her ninetieth birthday, we had a big party in Colorado, which her granddaughter Rebecca, herself an inveterate list maker, quietly organized. When Mom finally was told about the event, she rallied, enthusiastically planning and making lists for Maureen and Kathi to follow in getting her properly attired and all the way to Denver for the celebration.

By June, her health was failing rapidly, but she evidently wasn't quite through planning. There was a day when she was exceptionally spry and lucid, and Kathi and Maureen spent the day with her, laughing and sharing the fun.

The next day, a Thursday, after lunch, she asked Maureen, "Did you call Kathi?"

"No, why was I supposed to call Kathi?"

"Well, it's time for me to go."

Maureen, incredulous, called Kathi and told her what Mom had said. Neither of them took it completely seriously, but they both stayed closer. Late on Friday evening, with both of her daughters present, Kathi heard her cry out in prayer, and then she was quiet. Sometime that night, she had a massive stroke and passed into a coma.

Geraldine Byrda Payton Knight died on Tuesday, June 8, 2004, exactly on the anniversary of the passing of our dad, her husband, in 1987. Most of us have no doubt that she had planned it to the day. It was the last thing on her list.

Atmosphere at the Columbine Steakhouse

The neighborhood at Third and Federal in Denver is a collection of small used car lots on the verge of being junkyards, Asian food and mercantile stores, noodle shops, gas and convenience stores, nondescript commerce, and, on the corner, the Columbine Steakhouse. Established in 1961, it is a midcentury modern structure with a sweeping low roofline, massive wooden beams inside, and an atmosphere that fits the neighborhood.

The Columbine has been purveying baked potatoes and steaks, from filets to porterhouse, for over half a century. I had my first experience there when I joined my brother Jerry, his wife Rosie, and two children one Saturday evening in 1971. Just inside the front door, we encountered men in white aprons taking orders and barking them down the line. We made our selections from the illuminated movable-letter signboard suspended above and were handed a tray of salads in tan Bakelite bowls to be carried to any table of our choice.

The place was jumping that night, and adrenaline flowed through the room. It seemed like just minutes after our party of three adults and two small children had walked in and gotten situated that the burliest white apron brought our baked potatoes, burgers, and steaks and presented us with change for a twenty, correctly anticipating the amount to be tendered.

In the whirl and because of it, Jerry and I both dug in with a frenzy, finishing our salads, potatoes, and steaks in all of twelve minutes. The kids were not about to be rushed, and Rosie just watched us in amusement. I can't tell you whether my steak was good or bad, but it must have been tender because I certainly didn't take time to chew it.

After I rested my fork and knife, I surveyed the room. It was clean with well-trodden linoleum flooring and Formica tables. The tan salad bowls complemented platters in jade green. The forks were just strong enough to hold meat down for cutting with the black-handled steak knives. Maybe I exaggerate in calling it a dining experience, but the joint definitely had atmosphere.

The Columbine Steak House still operates on that corner in Southwest Denver, and it looks exactly like it did in 1971. I decided to have lunch there to see if it had changed. The highest price on the same old signboard, now much yellower, is for a porterhouse at about eighteen dollars. I noticed baked potatoes wrapped in foil and stacked by the grill. Salads were still coming out in tan Bakelite bowls, and the platters were still a jade green. I was not hungry enough for a steak, so I ordered a cheeseburger, and with fries and a coke, it came to seven bucks, including tax. I dropped two dollars in the tip jar, an extravagant 30 percent.

The pace seemed a bit more relaxed this time around, but then again, it was only noon on a Sunday. The burger was really quite good, finished over an open flame, and the fries were freshly cut. There were several patrons in Broncos jerseys, apparently bound for the game at Mile High north on Federal. Ceramic tile had replaced the linoleum floor, about the extent of any physical upgrade, except there is now a self-service soda dispenser over by the grill. It didn't ruin the atmosphere.

My Advanced Youth, the Early Stages

I am ready to admit that now, in my seventieth year, I am entering the early stages of advanced youth. I am excited to proceed because I understand it may be terminal, but it will not kill me. There are some things I escaped many years ago that I am happy won't be coming along. The stinging of iodine on a scratch comes to mind, as do spoonfuls of nasty castor oil for any sort of ailment.

And there are nice things that have fallen by the wayside I would like to take along, but can't, including a human-powered Royal typewriter, for instance, or Warner Brothers cartoons and double features at the movies. I would like to again be able to take trips to Grandma's.

Looking back, I am sorry I missed a whole list of events because I was born too late. How special it would be to have seen and carry with me recollections of America's big bands at the Trocadero Ballroom or Benny Goodman's famous Carnegie Hall concert or to have been part of the celebrations at the end of World War II.

There is another list of things I should be happy I missed, but part of me wishes I had been there, too. The Great Depression and Dust Bowl are experiences that nobody should have had to live through, but I would like to have been part of the resilient way in which our parents emerged to become the Greatest Generation, winning the wars in European and Pacific theaters.

I have been on this earth for the speeches and presidency of John Kennedy, the race for space, the Beatles, peace demonstrations, the eloquent struggles of Martin Luther King Jr., the computer age, sushi, and the speeches and presidency of Barack Obama. These memories I am happy to take into my seventies, but I must also carry along the sad thoughts of slaughters of children in their schoolhouses and young people killed *en masse* on their campuses and at the movies.

Youth is for learning new things and creating new memories. It is for making new friendships, doing new things, and going new places, and I will have it until I lose interest. It stops when I do.

As a new septuagenarian, I am still a proud father and

grandfather and part of a large, wonderful family, mostly Irish but with other rich strains running through. I still admire anything done with passion, whether it is an occupation, art, sport, or performance. I will continue to write and work, immerse myself in computers and gadgetry, travel, enjoy all the jazz music I can fit on my iPod, smile at the pretty girls, and fall in love at least once a week.

A Monkey Wrench in the Works

You will find a monkey wrench in the Grainger catalog with a price tag of over four hundred dollars. It is a high price, but then again, it's not something for your average toolkit unless you work on locomotives or with large industrial machinery. It is too cumbersome to drop in the pocket of your dungarees, and if you did, at eleven pounds, it would take your pants right down and ruin your suspenders.

The twenty-one inches of dropforged aluminum bronze are engineered for maximum leverage at the end of a burly arm and powerful grip. It has smooth, four-inch chops adjustable with a knurled screw to grasp a large, square nut. The cold and gray finish is nonmagnetic, nonsparking, and corrosion resistant. It meets the standards of the federal government, the military, OSHA, and several other agencies with less familiar acronyms. I have described a king-sized version, although there are monkey wrenches in the catalog where less bite and torque are specified.

A Baltimore mechanic named Charles Moncky is said to have invented the appliance in 1858. But similar tools were used on carriages in the century before that, and since the wrench mimics the open jaw of a monkey and not necessarily Charley, his claim on the name is uncertain. In a side note, a monkey wrench in Germany is colloquially called *Ein Engländer* or "an Englishman."

It is common for the unsophisticated to label all kinds of adjustable spanners as monkey wrenches, but they aren't if they don't have smooth jaws. Tried, true, and venerable monkey wrenches are still pulled out by mechanics, plumbers, and farmers determined to break loose old, rusted, nonstandard square nuts and bolts.

What really drew me to describe this engaging apparatus is not its heft or utility, but the phrase, "throw a monkey wrench in the works." I have learned that, in the early days of the industrial revolution, workers could get a brief respite from work in a hot, noisy factory by tossing in a monkey wrench to halt the machinery. Our English expression has a big sister in France and Europe in the word "sabotage," which is said to derive from workers throwing their wooden shoes, called *sabots*, into textile looms or the linkages of industrial machinery for a quick break from monotony or perhaps to make an anonymous statement against a despised supervisor.

Of the two expressions, the word "sabotage" rolls off the tongue, wins the linguistic efficiency award, and universally describes acts of gritty resistance. Saboteurs may be environmental activists, union firebrands, civilian rebels, or guerillas at war. Those are all dangerous and romantic occupations, to be sure, but I will leave them for others to pursue.

For me, I am still thinking about that $439 price tag and whether I can get by with a lesser model. Somehow, throwing a monkey wrench in the works seems more personal than sabotage. It is just you and me, angling for some time for a run to Starbucks.

THE DESPERATE DEED

The zenith of my acting career, in fact, the entirety of my acting career, came in 1957 in *The Desperate Deed* on the rattling wooden rollout stage of Saint Laurence School in Laramie. I was in the eighth grade, the highest level at our school, and it was a new work written and produced by our school's principal, the reverential but irreverent Sister Mary Sarah.

It was a turn-of-the-century melodrama replete with villain, damsel in distress, valiant hero (me), musical numbers by our school choir, and a Floradora dance line featuring boys dressed up like Mae West in gaudy and curvy costumes. I know Sister's casting choice was an example of her sense of fun because there were certainly girls available and they were prettier than we were.

I was one of the Floradora dancers early in the show, and then I had to make a quick costume change for my other role as the boy "detecative" (Sister's word) who rescued the lovely heroine and brought the villain to justice. I like to believe I was picked for my talent, but it likely was that I was the shortest boy in the room and could pass for a lad amid other fourteen-year-olds in roles of adults. My curly, dashing good looks were, of course, a bonus.

My friend Roger Morgan played the tall, mustachioed villain. The script dictated that, at the climactic moment when the scoundrel had me in his grasp to block the rescue, I would feint a stomp to his foot. Roger would howl, and with him in pursuit, I would dash off to free the lovely damsel just as she approached the screeching buzz saw. We practiced several times to perfect the stomp, dash, and rescue, but after the final dress rehearsal, I gleefully thought of a secret wrinkle.

The play went off brilliantly before a full house in the school gymnasium. The gay nineties songs were cheerful, the dancers were in step, the jokes were funny, and the audience was caught up in the drama. The suspense built through several acts right up to the instance of the feigned stomp when I instead delivered a crunching blow with everything I had directly to Roger's big toe.

Roger's howl exceeded all expectations, greatly entertaining the audience but startling our cohorts on stage and alarming Sister Mary Sarah in the wings. Roger lunged for my shoulder, I ducked and darted to the damsel in distress, and he hopped after me in pursuit. That hopping part was ad-libbed. He had never done it in rehearsal, and it was a nice touch. The audience loved it.

The show continued on script all the way to the happy ending, and we took bows to what I remember as a standing ovation. I believe I got the best laugh of the night, Roger got a purple toe award, and we both deserved best actor nominations.

Backstage after the curtain calls, Roger caught up to me for real, and I vainly tried to plead remorse while doubled in laughter. He wasn't sharing the mirth, but in retrospect, I would say he should have considered himself lucky for having survived the night. Sister might have written the play with a pistol in my hand.

Rolling in Rallods

I think of the counting room of a billionaire, there for him to roll through piles of stocks, bonds, and greenbacks, but is he enriched or enslaved? Is he secure in wealth or insecure in a mirage?

Then I think of the times I have found a twenty-dollar bill in the pocket of my blue jeans and I feel rich. I might blow it on a movie, a book, or a nice steak from the butcher shop, but it is not going in the bank.

The dollar is a poor way to measure true wealth. We are richest when we observe and engage in treasures that cannot be hidden in a safety deposit box or converted to some form of barter to be deposited, invested, accounted for, or worried about. What's more, these gifts come to us tax-free. We need a way to keep score of life's riches, so I propose we henceforth count them in terms of the "rallod," a new unit of currency represented not by a dollar sign but by a smiley face.

As I ponder this measurement to tabulate the joys of living, I sit at my window on a Sunday morning assessing the snowiest day of the year. I have evaluated the storm for beauty and benefits, adjusted for nuisance and inconvenience, and awarded myself five thousand rallods (☺5,000). And for braving its soft fury on the trail, I award myself another ten thousand. A woman on snowshoes just trundled by, and that vision is worth a thousand. If this was a workday and the office declared it a snow day, I'd give myself ten thousand more. You will notice you earn rather than pay to enjoy life, and inflation is not a problem.

Even though it's a winter day, my economic model is really all about stopping to smell the roses, and to that specific pleasure, I think we may assign a value by calculating a hundred rallods for each blossom you find on the bush and an extra fifty for every whiff you take. If you are enterprising, you may sniff your way through the neighborhood garden center and come out on the other end a billionaire. Then go home, cut the lawn, lie on it, inhale the new-mown fragrance, have a beer, and give yourself a 10 percent bonus.

My counting system is self-administered, and you won't need a CPA. Heck, you won't even need a wallet. You may accumulate rallods however you like and wallow in them like Scrooge McDuck, go out and earn some more, and fall asleep counting them. You should, of course, deduct for brief, unpleasant moments. For instance, driving past a feedlot in the country would cost you a thousand rallods, but you may recoup that loss by going straight to Dairy Queen.

I hope this summarizes my plan well and that all of you will adopt it as your own. Now go and gather rallods while ye may.

Yes, Dear

I was on the 3L eastbound on Alameda, a bus full mostly of office workers from downtown or Capitol Hill heading home in the afternoon rush hour. I had a window seat, hoping my beefy seatmate would be getting off first so I would not have to crawl over her.

I watched as a man in a dark suit and tie took the seat to my front left. He had a choice but selected to sit on the aisle, subtly blocking others from the window seat. Maybe he just did not want to rub butts and elbows with a stranger. I did not observe him listening to music or becoming engaged in conversation. He just looked straight ahead, anxious or dreading his destination.

I was relaxing in the peace and simple monotony of overheard conversation and engine and road noises amid infrequent stops along the lush residential stretches between Holly and Quebec when the most urgent of ringtones interrupted my reverie. I was among the dozen passengers nearby who grabbed for pockets and purses, grateful to discover it was not for me.

Baxter (I gave him a name), the man in the suit and necktie, answered the call. I could hear only his side of the dialog, which was minimal and infrequent, but if I was sitting closer to him, I might have even caught the other side. I can only tell you there were not many pauses, and the volume strained the cell phone as Baxter held it to his ear, sometimes close and sometimes a bit away.

For the purposes of this report, I will first tell you what I heard Baxter say, which wasn't much. "Hullo? Yes. I tried. No, dear. Yes, dear. Yes. No. Thank you. Yes, dear, I'll try again. Ten minutes. Okay. Yes, dear."

Now I will relate what I believe to be the specifics of what I didn't hear, basing it on my years of experience in the trenches of marital bliss. "You idiot. Did you forget you need to be home early? What do you mean you couldn't get out? Did you get that raise yet? Did you even ask for that raise yet? You know I can't get by on what you call a paycheck. I'm tired of the dollar store, and so is my mother. And speaking of mothers, did you even remember to call yours this morning? You know I need to borrow her curling iron. You don't know how lucky you are it's my mother who's living with us, not that battle-axe.

"Now it's going to be another ten minutes? You know Mother and I have bingo tonight, and we were counting on a nice early supper when you get home to fix it. But Mister Employee of the Month Who Can't Get a Raise misses his bus to stay behind and brownnose his lousy boss.

"By the way, Baxter, happy birthday."

My Father's Big Hands

From my father, I inherited broad shoulders and a mop that showed signs of silver by the time I was thirty. Like my brothers, I consider these gifts to be proud of. We look a lot like him, but none of us come close to having Dad's massive hands. The Union Pacific Railroad ring that marked his retirement in 1971 had to be specially crafted to fit a size seventeen, yet the big stone seemed dwarfed on his finger. They were handsome and functional hands, just very large.

He allowed that his mitts were handy for a boxer. He had done some prizefighting as a young man in Southern Colorado, and while I often assumed his hands had grown so large by training, a bit of research counters that they were that big when he finished growing. Nevertheless, I am sure the strength he built squeezing red rubber balls and handgrips made them formidable clubs.

Although he didn't have a long career in the ring, maybe eighteen bouts, Dad was proud of that phase of his life. Growing up, he was called by his given name of Emmett, but he became professionally known as the Fighting Mick, eventually even adopting the first name of Michael. He was Mike on the railroad and Mickey to our mother.

I remember many times as a young man sitting with Dad in his living room. I might have been reading or just enjoying the quiet peace when, across the room, Dad's big fingers would begin tapping out a tune. The strumming would continue for a while, and it almost always meant he was about to break into or whistle a song. It might have been a popular dance tune, an Irish ditty, or something from his Burl Ives repertoire, but I knew it was coming.

I often write humorously and unabashedly about my father because he was, by nature, a funny character who could laugh at himself. However, as I write these thoughts, I picture any one of his beautiful grandchildren clasped gently in his arms under a big, strong hand as he sings her a lullaby in quiet baritone. He loved them all, loved them equally, and recognized their uniqueness even as infants. He envisioned for them grand futures, and his dreams have been fulfilled again and again.

On May 4, 1987, I called to tell Dad about the birth of my second son, Robert Emmett Knight. Dad was thrilled to learn of the name we had chosen, telling me that Robert Emmett was a great hero and a martyr of the Irish revolution. Our Robert Emmett was the seventeenth and last of his grandchildren to be born.

That night, just hours after hearing my news, Dad was stricken by the abdominal aortic aneurism that took his life. He was rushed from Laramie to a hospital in Fort Collins with the facilities to treat him. He remained confined to the hospital but conscious for several weeks, and we received permission to take the baby to see him. He nestled Robert against his chest with that big right hand as his lips moved quietly in what I believe was an Irish lullaby. It was an indelible moment in my life.

I have one more story to relate to you that my sister Maureen told me this week. In his final days, Dad had lapsed into deep silence. Maureen was sitting at his side with her hand clasped in his. She spoke to him for a while, expecting no response until he squeezed lightly in answer and then tightly as she felt him pass his strength to her through the firm touch of that wonderful, big hand on hers. Today, she holds and touches her own six kids and many grandchildren at every opportunity, knowing she is in turn passing on to them the strength of her father and mine, Michael Emmett Knight, who died on June 8, 1987.

A One-Man Band Called Luigi

Even the name was an act because he was not an Italian named Luigi at all, but Ludvik Jurenic, a Serbian American who was born and lived his life in Butte, Montana. He was the proprietor of Luigi's Bar in the historic uptown business district on a hillside leaning tenuously against the void of Berkeley Pit, the world's largest open pit mine. Eventually, Lew moved his business and its unique assets down to Harrison Street, where it continued as a must-see destination for visitors and where I first met the establishment.

Lighted neon outside proclaimed Luigi and his Dancing Dolls, and inside Lew was Luigi, choreographer of his domain and a one-man band of twenty-four instruments. Exotic dolls, spinning ballerinas, clowns, monkeys, and puppets populated his walls. Geese flapped from the ceiling as bugs and spiders dropped on customers. An airplane zoomed across Luigi's sky, and in a corner sat Sally, a mannequin who might rise and flop about on any Luigi cue.

I can only wonder how many mischievous, gleeful hours Lew spent in the attic and basement stringing and organizing cables and counterweights that connected the puppets and everything else in his world to pedals that simultaneously crashed the cymbals, clapped the clappers, rang the cowbells, and drummed the drums. At his side was a xylophone, on his lap was a squeezebox, and hanging at his reach were levers, horns, and noisemakers. He wore zany hats and sometimes a skunk on his shoulder. It was a cacophony of sight and noise that might never have found a common beat but made a symphony.

Patrons soon learned they had better not go to the restroom while Luigi was on. The Him and Her doors were at opposite corners of the stage, and as soon as a him or her entered one, the polka would stop cold, and Luigi would heckle the poor absentee until she or he came out. Few would be gone (or should I say "be going") for long, and the dash back from john to barstool would be very quick. I know because I was a red-faced Luigi victim myself.

A teenaged Lew and his kid brothers had already formed an

accordion polka band when their young father died, and they earned money for the family at weddings and dances. They practiced in a hayloft with loose floorboards to which Lew nailed milk pails with rocks rattling in the bottom. When the boys tapped time, the pails played percussion. That was the genus and the genius of the one-man band called Luigi.

I lived and worked in Montana in 1969, but it was only long enough to get to Luigi's twice. The first was a busy Saturday night when the house was bouncing. The second was on a quiet weekday afternoon when I had the day off and I found Luigi affably pouring beers and enjoying his world. He played a set from his bandstand for the few patrons and later a tune with some brass bells he had lined up on the bar.

That afternoon, I met and chatted with his lovely wife, Pearl, who was the business brain and helped manage the fascinating eccentricities of her husband. I'm sure Luigi's Bar would never have made it without her.

There is much more to the seventy-seven years of Ludvik Jurenic, but I will conclude with the lyric of his life, which was Luigi's life, "Growing old is mandatory. Growing up is optional. Yabba Dabba Doo."

Space

I remarked to a good friend about the daunting task of writing on the subject of space and that it could mean anything from outer space to the space between your teeth. She laughed and recalled how her grandmother in Germany would tell her the space between her teeth meant she would see the world.

Space to grow and function is as necessary to a bee in a hive as it is to a pronghorn on the Wyoming plains. It is the canvas on which an eagle will soar and a rose will bloom.

Space is art. To an advertising designer, white space is magic to capture the eye. Artists brush positive and negative spaces into their masterpieces. Architects build with the same aesthetic. Photographers use space to frame their subjects.

Space is tempo. Poets punctuate with space and form. Composers imbue space into their music and call it rhythm. Who could ask for anything more? Frank Sinatra was known for his phrasing, which means he had command of space. "How deep is the ocean?" he sang. "How high the moon?" Both are matters of space.

Space is place and sequence. Envision a silent Charlie Chaplin creating a story without props in the space of an empty back lot. Alfred Hitchcock could deftly space characters in a scene to tell us how one relates to the other or terrorize us with the simple space of a bloody shower floor. Think of Jack Benny provoking extra laughs by inserting a drawn-out space of silence in his delivery.

Space is mathematics. A geometry student uses pi to calculate space in a circle. In industry, without space factored into the progression, Fords would crash on the assembly line. A farmer spaces seeds in rows aligned to make space for tractor wheels. Tractors cultivate a field plotted mathematically to optimize use of space and to take advantage of gravity, which is yet another function of space.

Space is safety. Controllers in towers monitor and keep spaces between airplanes. On the ground, the space you keep between yourself and the car ahead may be the space between life and death.

Space is motion. A basketball team uses space to create offense and frustrate defense. In baseball, the fortunes of pitcher and batter rest on one creating space and the other closing space between bat and ball. Football players close space or use it for separation. Cyclists, runners, and swimmers manage their own relationships to space. Space to a boxer may be the difference between a knockout and a glove held high in triumph. A jockey maneuvers for space on the outside to ride her colt to victory.

Space is personal. We make space in our home for company and find a private space for solitude. We have space in our heart for loved ones and save some of it for ourselves. We keep space from strangers but let it be a space for friendship to grow.

Space is serenity. A quiet space in the forest gives way to a waterfall. A Japanese gardener uses space to show balance in nature, and in the same vein, the Chinese have given us feng shui, using space to create harmony in our homes and offices. A sunbeam and a tabby find each other in a space by the window.

The beauty of space lies in its discovery. I shall keep exploring the crannies and occupy, for as long and as respectfully as I may, my own little space in this amazing continuum.

Murder by Mary McGuire

She booted the Apple, opened a blank page, centered the cursor at the top, and typed the word "Murder." It was a fine, unadorned title for a sure-to-be best seller. She added her byline and declared it a good start.

She wanted a captivating opening paragraph, considering fragments and combinations of phrases, but found them all either weak or wacky. After several minutes, she rolled away from the keyboard and decided a short break would spur the process. She clicked Save, preserving her work-in-progress, and congratulated herself. Mary McGuire had indeed started on her goal of writing the great American mystery. She then went to the kitchen and resumed pursuit of another of her life's goals, to brew the great American cup of coffee. That was seven years and thousands of pots ago.

In the interim, along came Romeo. He courted Mary for months, doting on her Irish eyes and drinking her coffee by the gallon. They were attorneys and rising stars both, governmental affairs for him and intellectual property law for her. After their marriage, they rented a suite for their separate practices in a converted mansion in Denver's Capitol Hill district. It was a nice arrangement, sharing a secretary and a coffee maker and riding the light rail together almost every day.

Mary's law practice was quiet and cerebral, involving patents, trade secrets, and the technical, as well as registering and defending copyrights in the creative fields of music, art, literature, and software applications. It could be rough and tumble on occasion, but ultimately, it was sanely centered on who came first and proof thereof.

Mary took vicarious pleasure in hearing Romeo tell of his exploits and the players in the state government and later in the corridors of Washington. He thrived in the industry of regulatory government, one that celebrated the art of spin and skirted the weight of law. He was a lobbyist whose work focused on influencing power and policy in minerals, oil, and gas. He had talent for persuasion and knew where the skeletons were hung and where the skids needed greasing. He earned far more than any elected official did.

As time went along and Romeo achieved even more success, so also was his work more often centered in Washington, and travel became more frequent. Earlier this year, he flew off to meet a senator and his aide concerning some sort of exploration in the tropics. It was a trip that consumed Romeo for several weeks, and he made very little contact with home.

Travel then became even more frequent, and the durations grew longer. He finally came home from a long one last Friday, walking in the door only hours after she opened the letter from his attorney. So now that you know where this is going, I will jump straight to the epilogue.

On Sunday morning, Mary brewed a fresh pot of strong coffee, booted her computer, located her nascent piece in the archives, and opened it for the first time in seven years. She had a story now, and under the existing title and byline she typed it, chapter by chapter, through the night until it reached a conclusion captured in two bittersweet and very final words, "The End."

This morning, she posted a copy of the manuscripts of *Murder by Mary McGuire* to Random House and another to the Denver Police Department and caught the next flight to Madagascar where they grow great coffee beans and do not extradite.

What I Missed in Kindergarten

All I Really Need to Know I Learned in Kindergarten was published in 1988 and was updated and released again in 2013 as an anniversary edition. It's a compilation of essays by Robert Fulghum telling us about the world in five hundred-word bursts. He would fit nicely in my writing circle because that's what we do, and while we might not have access to his millions of readers, he would be a nice role model.

Today, the task is a composition on the subject of "grade school," and I have been thinking about Fulghum's book and wishing I had had the inspiration first. It's based on a simple idea that we learned in kindergarten everything we need to know about how to live, what to do, and how to be, things like sharing everything, playing fair, not hitting people, cleaning up your own mess, flushing, and taking a nap every afternoon. A few other tenets round out his list, and then the book subsumes about seventy delightful essays on life and people who were apparently paying attention when they were five.

I will take the opposite tack and tell you not what I learned in kindergarten but some things I needed to know but didn't learn in kindergarten. For instance, where was my vaunted kindergarten education in 1978 when I changed the alternator on my Mercury Zephyr on a very cold winter morning? I tightened the last bolt, set the wrench down somewhere, and fired her up. As the car idled, suddenly said tool hit the fan (I paraphrase) and put a gash in the radiator. I learned that jugs of stop-leak compound poured into a radiator with a hole the size and shape of a wrench will not get you far. With those chemicals and extra gallons of antifreeze, I just made it to a radiator shop, leaving a fluorescent green trail all the way.

I have reviewed Fulghum's credo, and maybe I should not blame the radiator fiasco on kindergarten because we actually were taught to put things back where we found them. And to his credit, I know the radiator man remembered another kindergarten lesson to not take things that aren't yours because I got the wrench back but with sarcasm, which he also probably learned in kindergarten.

I cannot blame a teacher's lapse for my next tale of woe because dishwashers weren't part of life in 1948, and it wasn't until I got my first apartment in 1964 that I learned the hard way not to put liquid dish soap in a dishwasher. Now how illogical is that? The result was a spectacular, floating bubble bath in my kitchen. I slid around the linoleum and finally got the flow stanched before it took the living room.

I learned suds are not Lawrence Welk bubbles. They are mostly water, and they do not just pop and evaporate. I heard the voice of my kindergarten teacher scolding me, "Clean up your own mess." I did so. Then I remembered one other thing she taught us, and I took a nap.

THE LITTLE WHITE CHURCH IN VIRGINIA DALE

A frontier cemetery rambles at her side with finely engraved markers set amid rough boards and crude stones scratched or chiseled to identify the resident. Many are so old that they cannot be read.

It is a tidy sanctuary with five pews on the left and four and a half on the right. The short one makes space for a woodstove near the middle but keeps the center aisle clear for a proper wedding procession. The white pulpit fronts an altar elevated slightly to be just that much closer to heaven. An organ, chair, and two flags occupy the rest of the stage in front of the cross on the wall. A vestibule provides transition to and from the weather. You'll not find a temple or cathedral more important to a community and a single young visitor than the little white church in Virginia Dale, Colorado.

She was built in 1880, a few miles up the valley, and in 1884, in the middle of the night during a feud within the congregation, she was hauled to a creek downhill from the Virginia Dale stage stop. In the early days, she was Methodist and then Presbyterian for a while, but mostly she has been a simple community church. Regular services are monthly, and people often choose her for weddings, baptisms, and funerals.

Her doors are never locked, and for a century and a quarter, she has provided shelter to stranded travelers by horseback, wagon, and automobile. She asks no questions, seeks no alms, keeps firewood in the stove, and provides a clean, dry place to sit or sleep and wait out the storm. There is even an outhouse in the back.

She is a phoenix. In 2003, an arsonist, a young volunteer fireman with a fascination for flame, interrupted her life. She burned to the ground, but she did not succumb. Donations came from far and near, an architect created construction drawings pro bono, tradesmen volunteered skills, and others gave their time and energy. Just two months after the blaze, her shiny, new doors opened again for worship, community meetings, and, as always, respite for the weary. There was enough money left to create a trust for her upkeep.

The little white church in the dale took on a new meaning to my family recently. My brother Jim helps out every year with a music festival in Laramie. He sometimes takes artists to and from various locations, and on the week of the 2012 festival, he drove a young performer from Oakland who told him she had just recently broken a marriage engagement. Her fiancé had often spoken about getting married in a special little white church he knew in Colorado.

Jim, knowing this was the place and that it would be open, took her there. The girl sat quietly by the stove with her guitar, finally asking with her eyes if it would be all right. And with Jim's nod, she sang an old blues standard, "Trouble in Mind." She finished, reflected a bit, and then stepped as a phoenix from that little white church in the vale into a rainbow of hope bright on the ridge ahead.

UNCLE JOYCE KILGORE

You probably have never heard of Singletree, Wyoming, so I'll tell you about it. My great uncle, Joyce Kilgore, then seventy years of age, had won a half acre of rangeland in a poker game down in Colorado. It had on it a big cottonwood tree and what was optimistically called a pond, and it was alongside where they would be putting in the new transcontinental railroad. It was the opportunity Uncle Joyce and Aunt Willie (Wilhelmina) had been awaiting, the chance to build a fine saloon and a source of income for their waning years.

Willie saw the cottonwood as a lightning rod that would get them killed, and she was all for chopping it down and sawing it into planks for the new business. But Joyce liked the shade and thought it would be an asset, so he rode back to Colorado territory, won a cart in another poker game, piled it high with lumber and nails, brought the load back to Wyoming, parked it under the tree, and went to work.

By June of 1868 steel for the new railroad was being laid down at the rate of a mile a day over Sherman Hill and onto the Laramie Plains. It was soon within sight of the brand-new Singletree Saloon standing proud by the pond in the shade of that voluminous old cottonwood.

It had a dirt floor, a fairly effective roof, barrels for stools, and a long, rough-hewn bar. The bottles on the back wall were well out of reach of railroad rowdies with arms stretched longer by the plying of sledgehammers. There was even a room in the back with a lace curtain for living quarters.

For two weeks, Joyce and Willie raked in more money than they had ever known. End-of-rail soon moved west, shutting off the bonanza, but the bar still drew folks in from the ranches, out from Laramie, and up from Virginia Dale.

They installed a wooden floor for dancing and felt quite established in business, but they were not yet a dot on any map, so they incorporated themselves as the town of Singletree, Wyoming. Willie got herself appointed postmistress, and Joyce elected himself mayor and poet laureate.

On the face of a sandstone tablet, our newly official bard chiseled out two lines, "Ain't no pome will ever be, as purty as this here tree." He leaned it against the cottonwood. Next, Joyce planted along the side of the road a succession of five wooden signs that read, in turn, "Yer gettin' near, our purty tree, have a beer, and take a pee. Singletree Saloon." Burma Shave never did it better.

Business flourished, and Uncle Joyce Kilgore soon added more tables and chairs, along with another, larger room in the back with a private kitchen for Wilhelmina.

It was August 1888 when the wind came up and the sky darkened. Just as the rain started, a single bolt of lightning wiped out the mighty cottonwood in a crashing instant, leveling with it the Singletree Saloon.

It was the demise of Uncle Joyce and Aunt Willie and the destiny she had feared for twenty years. Their graves were marked and the saloon memorialized only by that tablet still leaning against the stump of the mighty cottonwood. The tablet has since crumbled to sand, and the dot on the map called Singletree is no longer.

Today, as you drive north out of Colorado onto the Laramie Plains, you will see neither Singletree nor a single tree. A smokestack will eventually come into view, telling you civilization is ahead, but first watch the side of the road. You might see a grassy pond and faded boards inviting you to stop, have a beer, and relieve yourself. You may still do that, but you won't find a single tree to go behind.

WORRY AND WONDER

The challenge is to write on the subject of worry versus wonder, so naturally I have worried all week about wonder and wondered all week about worry. They are similar states of mind, but I believe the distinction of hope sets them apart. You can worry about life in a vicious cycle or wonder about life in the hope of a new tomorrow.

The saga of a misplaced set of car keys begins with wondering why they are not where they should be, and after checking and rechecking all the usual places, wonder becomes worry. Into what grated storm drain could they have fallen, and how might they be replaced in time to get to work?

Sometimes, you might even worry that the keys have been lifted and the car has been stolen, but you keep looking until you finally find them deep in the pocket of yesterday's trousers. As worry relaxes into wonder, yet another worry pops up, this one about the state of your mind, but you are mobile again so now you can just worry about traffic.

Back in 1988, at a time when I was keeping problems of my own from everyone, it seemed hourly the radio played a popular new song, "Don't Worry, Be Happy." It was a peppy and irritatingly contrary reminder that I indeed did have plenty to worry about. It made Bobby McFerrin famous and showed the world his genius, but it left me resentful for decades.

Every attempt I have made at writing this essay brings me straight to someone whom I consider a best friend. We often tease him about it, but for more than sixty-five years, he has represented to me the very embodiment of a capacity for unabashed wonder. Every waterfall, bridge, canyon, or birdsong impresses him as being the most beautiful thing on the planet. It is the rare café discovered in our travels that fails to serve him the best breakfast he has ever had. If he has a fault, it is in a generosity that extends far, wide, and without reserve. He has lately found himself feeling alone and in a state of deep personal worry. He is not himself, and for that, we worry, too.

There is no advice more meaningless and less welcome than when someone, even Bobby McFerrin, tells you not to worry and be happy. Reflecting on my own crisis, however, I now realize there was some truth to the silly song because worry itself was fixing nothing. It was not even forestalling the predicaments of my worrying. Worry had me incapacitated in its grip.

Wonder and hope and maybe even faith, like that set of missing car keys, is tucked into some hidden pocket of your mind and soul, but you have to keep searching because, as Mom told me often, it will always be in the last place you look.

Blue

More than half the flags of the world feature the color blue, including Old Glory. *Our Flag*, a book published by Congress in 1879, reports the color in our flag has no meaning, but that in our Great Seal, it represents vigilance, perseverance, and justice.

In Washington, blue suits are often the only common thing between any two legislators or bureaucrats, liberal or conservative, woman or man. And in the corporate world, executives often wear blue suits to show gravitas for business at hand. For several years in the eighties, I recruited candidates for a management consulting firm that required their engineers to wear white shirts and reliable, responsible blue suits, period.

Marketing managers employ the color blue to convey strength and trust. Ford, Facebook, American Express, Chase, GE, and even IBM ("Big Blue" itself) have structured their corporate images around the color. Kmart's latest logo contains an image of their famous blue light. A few years ago, Kmart Holdings acquired Sears, whose logo, as you probably remember, is also blue. From the performance of the blended companies, do not be surprised if they soon put a blue light special out on the whole sorry outfit, maybe some kind of a BOGO deal.

A member of the nobility often is called a blue blood, but we know blood is not blue at all. It is red because of oxygen and hemoglobin. It is red in the veins, arteries, and heart, and it stays that color even when you die. Therefore, if some fancy pants aristocrat is in fact blue-blooded, we can agree it is an oxygen deficiency.

The sky seems blue because of wavelengths, scattering, and things that have to do with the sun, nature, and even altitude. Science notwithstanding, if you think the sky needs a color boost, you can always cuss up a blue streak yourself or delegate the chore to a gaggle of teenagers.

Does hearing the melody "Blue Skies" bring to mind bluebirds singing their song? And how does that cheerful image square with that of another piece, "I've Got a Right to Sing the Blues"? This gamut of emotion is depicted in Vincent Van Gogh's masterpiece, "Starry Night." In billowing swirls of atmosphere and brilliant stars, the soaring blue of optimism and the deep blue of melancholy can together fill a soul.

But there I go, getting philosophical again, and I've promised to control that vice. I will make you a deal. Let's pack a picnic basket. I will bring the Blue Ribbon beer, and you can pack your blueberry pie. We'll fly Jet Blue off into the wild blue yonder and spend the day in a blue lagoon under the blue sky and watch blue herons in flight as the sun goes down over the blue Pacific. Later, I'll sweep you off to the Blue Paradise Ballroom where we'll dance the Blue Tango until we're blue in the face. But, please, don't step on my blue suede shoes.

Labor Day Is for the Bees

"I've got a writing job for you, pal. Are you interested?" It was a strange voice disturbing my Sunday slumber with a speech impediment I could not quite place, but it seemed he buzzed through his esses. He droned on. "I know you're there, buddy, and you claim to be a writer, so wake up and listen."

And there he was on my knee, gazing up and over the mound of my waistline. Fully reclined and trapped in my La-Z-Boy, I could not lift my head enough to see him except by rolling my eyes downward. I was at the mercy of a yellow menace with a stinger.

"Gompers is the name, and honey's my game. We have been reading some of your stuff down at AHMPA, and you're just the boy for this job. Things are getting real bad for my courageous brothers and sisters of the Amalgamated Honey Makers and Pollinators of America, and we need some fancy new slogans for our picket lines."

I certainly did not have fancy language for a bunch of crabby honeybees with picket signs. Of course, I always respected their work and thought it might be the most important job on earth, pollinating the blossoms that mature into the grasses and fruits and vegetables that feed the world and, after all that, making nice honey for my biscuit.

Suddenly, I felt sympathetic. "Okay, Mr. Gompers, I'll give it a try. What are you looking for?"

Gompers let me get up from the recliner, and then, buzzing around, he herded me to my desk.

"Labor Day's coming up, and every year at this time, we hear stories about working men and women, how they struggle, how they build societies, and how they yearn for a better life. They have been getting all the attention, but now it's time for a rising of the honeybees. We need you to cook up some hot new slogans to buzz up our membership, shake the world, and swat down the capitalist beekeepers."

I clicked the mouse, and as my computer woke from its nap, I booted my own brain and waited for words to flow. I was used to this predicament because it struck me every Sunday night with a Monday morning writer's deadline looming.

"Okay, here's one. How about Buzzing for Bees?"

Gompers twisted the tip of his wing into the shape of a thumb, pointed it down, and buzzed a profanity.

"All right then. How about Buzzing for Justice?"

"Stronger, man. Stronger."

We went back and forth with iterations that included demands for better working conditions, less power to the queen, production bonuses, more space in the hive, wing therapy, and reduced flight time. We even pondered threats of stinger attacks and nectar sabotage.

Finally, the sweet, perfect sequence came together and fancier words have never before been seen or heard in the history of world labor movements. "Love Your Local Honeybee, or Go Pollinate Yourself."

STILL GROWING UP

Right at birth, we are handed the task of growing up. Most of us reach our maximum height by the time we are about twenty, and by default, we fall into that category of humans called the grown-ups. At that point, we are expected to demonstrate mature behavior, participate in society, and, if we produce children, raise them to become successful grown-ups themselves. Sometimes we do these things well and sometimes not so well.

Ask me if I am a grown-up, and I will tell you no. I am happily still in the process, and please do not expect me to get there too soon. As long as I am learning, I am still in the business of growing up.

There are plenty of models for me to follow in this quest. Laura Ingalls Wilder had a lifetime of teaching, which necessarily also involved a lifetime of learning. She did not publish the first of her *Little House* books until she was in her late sixties, and she was inspired to that by learning from her own daughter's budding writing career.

Frank McCourt was born in Brooklyn in 1930 in the throes of the Great Depression, but he was raised in Ireland after the family returned to the old country, only to sink more deeply into poverty and the dysfunction of an alcoholic father. His schooling ended at age thirteen, and he helped his mother and siblings survive by hook and by crook. He connived his way back to America six years later, and at twenty-one, he was drafted into the Korean War. He eventually used his GI Bill and, without the prerequisite of a high school diploma, talked his way into the prestigious New York University. By the age of twenty-seven, he was a teacher. At age sixty-six, he wrote and published his memoir, *Angela's Ashes*, for which he received a Pulitzer Prize.

Anna Mary Robertson Moses was born in 1860, married in 1887, and lived on a farm in Virginia. She had ten children, five of whom died at childbirth. At the age of seventy-six and crippled with arthritis, she gave up embroidery and began to paint. Grandma Moses may have lacked technical expertise, but her works are folksy and colorful masterpieces created from the fabric of a lifetime of learning.

My personal role model is a man who joined my circle of writers just a couple years ago at the age of ninety-five. He claims never to have written at all, yet he is a powerful wordsmith who has just begun to write down in beautiful pieces the journal of a long life. I know we will have learned something new and grown just a little more whenever Mike reads us one of his articles, and I believe he gets the same from the rest of us. There is no better example than that of a man who is still growing up as he approaches the milestone of a hundred years in the process.

An Open Letter to Newton Minow

Dear Mr. Minow,

Back in 1961, after President Kennedy made you chairman of the Federal Communications Commission, you told executives in the television industry, "When television is good, nothing is better ... but when television is bad, nothing is worse." You invited them to keep their eyes glued to their own stations for a full day and night until signoff. "I can assure you," you said, "that what you will observe will be a vast wasteland."

The television folks took a dig back at you with a show featuring seven castaways who landed on *Gilligan's Island* in the wreckage of a bucket the producers gleefully christened the *SS Minnow*. The series is still in its fifth decade of reruns out in the vastness of the wasteland.

As head of the FCC, you pointed the industry in a direction that grew from perhaps five stations serving a metropolitan area to hundreds of channels today, but I doubt even you could have anticipated the colorful images in brilliant high definition now splashing across giant screens in our homes.

A recent phenomenon that has taken the industry is reality television. The best of it includes programs like *Antiques Roadshow* and *This Old House* on public television. I like *American Pickers* on the History Channel about a couple of dudes finding treasure in other people's trash. Another show on that network called *Pawn Stars* has lowbrow characters who irritate me to no end, but their customers and the fascinating things they bring in the door have me watching.

For twenty-five years, *Cops* has taken audiences along on real police rides, showing us the world and the people they face from their viewpoint. There are other television series about unique folks who live, function, and survive in dangerous places. You may wonder just how a camera happens always to be in the right place to capture the action, but sometimes watching the tube requires a leap of faith. I remember making the same compromise to follow Marlin Perkins on *Wild Kingdom* back in 1963.

I happily avoid programs like "real" housewives degrading themselves in New Jersey or Beverly Hills, and I vow never to watch what I imagine must be the worst thing to ever wander into the wasteland. *Here Comes Honey Boo Boo* is said to be about a precocious monster of a little girl in the world of child beauty contests, where toddlers and primary grade children, exploited by parents living vicariously through their daughters, parade in heavy makeup and grown-up clothing, sometimes with strategic padding, and coached to take provocative poses. The fact that it is shown on The Learning Channel is sadly ironic.

So, Mr. Minow, I must report, with the number of choices in the half century having multiplied by some thirty times, nothing has changed. The best prove that, when television is good, nothing is better, but there is still plenty of bad, and the wasteland is vaster. It's a perfect landscape to introduce my idea for a reality series about my own life. I'm calling it *Denny Boo Booed*.

Trust Me

Do you remember O. J. Simpson dashing through the airport to reach the rental counter before somebody else got to that SUV? Hertz paid him for this endorsement. Years later Simpson got Ford free nationwide airtime in live aerial images of a long police chase of a white Bronco up and down the freeways of Los Angeles. That was when Simpson learned he was about to be arrested for a double murder. He beat that rap, but he has been in more trouble since. Hertz does not call him anymore, and neither does Ford.

I have never been in the market for a hair extension, but had I been, I certainly would have paid attention to Paris Hilton's commercials for Dream Catchers. A beneficiary of the massive Hilton Hotels fortune, the spoiled brat has since been in trouble for drunk driving, speeding, driving without a permit, and even shoplifting. Her Dream Catchers are on parole.

We admired the remarkable endurance of Lance Armstrong, who survived cancer and won the Tour de France a record seven times. He became a trusted world hero and a spokesperson for many brands, including Trek Bicycle, 24-Hour Fitness, and Anheuser-Busch, all the while denying, deflecting, and trivializing allegations of using performance-enhancing drugs. Recently the US Anti-Doping Agency brought irrefutable proof he had done so throughout his career. When he finally admitted it, sponsors cancelled millions of dollars in endorsement deals.

Oscar Pistorius, who lost his lower legs before his first birthday, inspired the world by winning gold as the courageous "Blade Runner" in the Paralympics and gained his greatest fame as a viable competitor in the 2012 London Olympic Games. He had contracts worth more than two million a year with Nike, Oakley Sunglasses, and important European corporations, but he lost them all after facing charges for the alleged Valentine's Day murder of his famous model girlfriend. We have allowed these celebrities and others like them to tell us what, when, and where to buy things, and they have let us down.

The late Billy Mays was the unchallenged king of OxiClean and countless other "as seen on TV" products. People seem to take to pitchmen like him because they bring such urgency to the moment, implying only a limited availability of the product. Yet, if you let the offer go unheeded, you can be sure that the infomercial will appear again tomorrow with the same urgency, the next day, the next week, and for months ever after on that station and ten others.

But wait! It is time for a new face, and trust me on this folks. The ideal spokesperson for anything you can name is plain old me. I will bring my deep voice. "At General Electric, progress is our most important product." Here is another. "See your Chevy dealer today and test drive a shiny new Stingray. It's precision that knows no equal."

And here's the one that will nail my own career in the genre of product pitching. "Don't change that dial, friends! Trust me on this. I am here to tell you about the most exciting product ever. It's the incredible Thigh Master."

But wait, there's more ...

A Gobbled History of the Turkey

We can blame Christopher Columbus because he concluded in 1492 that he had landed in the East Indies when it was actually the Eastern seaboard islands of the Americas. Then, to compound it, he labeled the indigenous people who were there to meet him as Indians. Those of us who came to the continent in the explorer's wake are perpetuating the misidentification to this day, so I guess we are not too bright either.

The turkey got its name because of an extension of that same Columbus goof, or a very similar error. In 1523, an expedition of Spanish conquistadors to Mexico found specimens of *meleagris gallopovo*, a fowl native only to North America, and carried them back to the Eastern Mediterranean where the species was quickly domesticated. Then, in the decade beginning in 1550, British traders in the Med acquired livestock of the bird, believing it to be a species native to the country of Turkey. Hence, the word "turkey" landed in the English dictionary with a real turkey of an etymology.

In the meantime, back in Turkey, they call it the *hindi*, which means "bird of India." Has anything ever been more bassackward? In enlightened North America today, we call our own native bird the turkey because England thought it came from Turkey, and Turkey all the while thought it came from India. It all started with Columbus landing seven thousand miles off base and becoming a national hero in the doing.

The fatted turkey soon competed with the fatted goose as a mainstay of Christmas dinners throughout Europe and in the New World, which seems to have inherited the European talent for reaching errant conclusions that never get corrected.

Although the earliest known Thanksgiving celebration in our country was in Jamestown, Virginia in 1607, schoolchildren are taught incorrectly that the first Thanksgiving was held in 1621 at Plymouth, Massachusetts. Today, schoolchildren recreate a famous but inaccurate painting of that event, errantly portraying Pilgrims wearing the hats of Puritans, which they were not, and their friends, the Wampanoag people, in the headdress of tribes from the Great Plains, a thousand miles distant.

According to a *New Yorker* article in 1962, it is actually a myth that Ben Franklin espoused the turkey as our national bird, but he did pen a letter to his daughter declaring, "For my own part I wish the Bald Eagle had not been chosen the Representative of our Country. He is a Bird of bad moral Character." He explains his point in too many words for this essay, but he concludes by saying the turkey is the more respectable of the birds and though a "little vain and silly, a bird of courage."

Sometime in the past century, the word "turkey" in a Broadway review came to mean a bad show. When or how it became a put-down, I do not know, but I do hope that negative connotation excludes the wild turkey of America I admire.

In the meantime, out on the farm, while animal scientists have been developing domesticated turkeys with bigger, fatter, and juicier breasts, they have been shrinking their brains. Turkeys.

A Fly in the Oval Office

On his desk were briefs yet to read after another long, busy day in the Oval Office. It had been a stream of hobnobbing, moments with staff, and ceremonial events with citizens of all backgrounds, from children to mayors to war heroes. It had also been a day of ducking incoming grenades and lobbing them back at a Congress he had often scolded as recalcitrant.

Recalcitrant? Now that's just too polite. Constipated would be more like it.

The chief executive reflected on matters of politics and state as he put up his feet and leaned back in the comfortable old chair that has served presidents since JFK. It squeaked in protest.

Wonder what the Speaker would say if I oiled this thing?

Chuckling at his private joke, he sensed himself dozing off. Blinking to fight off sleep, his eyes focused on a spot on the wall left of the Rockwell painting. It was a big old fly.

Now, how did that thing get in here?

The fly flitted about the big room and alighted on the presidential blotter.

Sit there, bugger, and let me get a look at you. You got a microphone? A camera? Did Moscow send you? Nah, you're just a fly, but how'd you get in here? Was it one of the girls?

The head of state put down his feet, squared around, and reached across his desk. The fly retreated to a bust of Lincoln as the president picked up a report, a small one of thirty pages, and tried to get to work. It was one of those rare moments of distraction when words on paper refused to register in his mind.

That stupid bug is hiding, but he is in here. Is he over there on the Remington bronze? In the apple bowl? Is there a fly swatter in here?

The president opened drawers and doors of the majestic old desk and searched the room, looking behind drapes and checking secret doors, nooks, and crannies. It is a masterpiece of design, the Oval Office, with windows and a door opening out to the Rose

Garden, built-in bookcases, a fireplace, handsome furniture, and tasteful furnishings, but nary a fly swatter.

If he were to get any work done tonight, the fly had to go. He rolled the report in his hand into a weapon, set his jaw, and began to stalk his prey. The fly played with him, landing here and there, always within a swat's reach, but always just escaping until a solid Whap! cut the air and a floral arrangement tumbled to the carpet.

Then, as it had in his elections, the game finally tilted solidly in his favor. With his opponent now cornered in the famously cornerless room, the president paused, thought about the fly's daring courage, and reconsidered.

Okay, Mr. Fly, you are mine now, but I'm giving you a presidential pardon. When I open this door to the Rose Garden, you will be free to fly away, but do me a favor. There is a fellow over in the Senate ...

A Grumpy Old Imaginer

If it had just been he and his pals, it would have gone unnoticed, but there were women in his group that morning. And although technically the dictionary says the word can refer to persons of either sex, what there was left of the hair on his head stood on end when the breezy waitress yelled across the café, "Is everything great for *you guys* this morning?"

A testy retort caught in his wheezy old breath, and she was out of sight before he could reach his cane. Curtis realized he would soon qualify for the old scout badge of curmudgeon, and he would gladly pin it to his suspenders.

If the badge is a license to be a grumpy old man, he could do it with alacrity, and you had better watch out. He could tolerate such tokens of advancing age, but he would resist any expectation to capitulate to them. In fact, he was still working on a far more important symbol of his lifetime, the lofty badge of imaginer.

He thought again about the role of imagination and remembered when Lewis Carroll took him through the looking glass to see Wonderland. Theodor Seuss Geisel feted him with green eggs and ham, and Frank Baum delivered him to Oz via the tornado express.

Even as a first grader seven decades ago, Curtis would get so deeply and quietly lost in imagination that his teacher would have to touch his shoulder to draw him back. Adults called it daydreaming, a term he learned when his parents came back from parent-teacher conferences. The trait possessed him then as it would for a lifetime, and mere parental nagging would not discourage it.

Curtis could be happy reading clouds in the sky or dreaming of rainbow trout swimming in deep pools at the edge of a mountain stream. This morning, he reflected on the optimism of another imaginer, Martin Luther King Jr., and how his dreams sprouted and grew over decades into the election of the first black president of the United States. Great things can come from great imaginations. Curtis let his daydreams flow on.

Imagine a society safe enough to walk in.

Gunpowder should be for fireworks in the sky, ammunition for sport, weapons for law enforcement, and national defense, and that is about it. Is there comfort or discomfort in knowing guns may be concealed in the purses, pockets, or glove compartments of anonymous people? Even if they happen to be perfectly legal? Or not?

Imagine a climate healthful enough to grow in.

The rule has always been so obvious. Use but don't abuse. But mankind has abused, and now it falls to us to manage and nurture what is left. Imagine the possibilities if we do not.

Imagine a world without want.

Couldn't the very rich realize even higher success by empowering those who struggle? And do it freely and without judgment for the rightness of it and not just for the tax deduction?

And imagine a world without war.

What would happen if ideological, religious, and nationalist zealots who monger war for profit and power could imagine what they might gain from waging peace?

Curtis reached for his coffee. It was cold. His companions had left the café, and the waitress was nowhere in sight. When the skeptical, old agnostic realized he had spent another morning in his imagination, it cast him off on yet another thing to ponder.

Is this what they call prayer?

Christmas Magic and How I Survived It

December 25

It was a lovely Christmas morning, Aunt Maggie, but Sarah, I, and the children missed having you this year. Little Sally was thrilled with the Magic Bake Oven you sent. She must have produced at least eight batches of cookies today, and I expect she will soon get them right. And Ronny loves his Junior Magician kit. He has been reading and practicing all day, and I believe he is going to become quite the prestidigitator. In the meantime, my razor has disappeared, apparently forever.

The holidays are just not the same without you, Auntie, but I understand your misgivings about being around the children after your unexpected haircut three years ago and your broken nose last year. Perhaps Sally was a bit too young then for a Missy Miss Hair Salon Kit, and of course, none of us knew the power of Ronnie's punch until he laced on those Rocking Rocky boxing gloves.

December 28

Ronald has already mastered his magic tricks and demonstrates every one of them over and over and over, and he is learning the irritating banter of an illusionist. More things are missing, and into the wizard's limbo today went my favorite Mel Tormé CD to follow my Norelco, nail clippers, and brush.

Sally still does not have the hang of baking, but she's persistent, and I've made three trips to the toy store for replacement mixes at about five bucks a pop. Is that not pretty high, Auntie? Her cookies come out shiny, so I plan to increase the oven temperature by putting a bigger light bulb in the socket.

December 29

I should have checked the warning label. The hundred-watt bulb warped the side of Sally's oven, and now her cookies are burning, but at least her cakes are not soupy.

By the way, could you tell me please where you purchased the magic set? I am hoping the company might have a different model, one that will help me reverse some of those spells.

December 30

I have just a short note today, Auntie. I cannot eat another burned cookie, and if one more thing of mine disappears, I swear I'm going to take that fake silk hat and cram it right over the little sorcerer's ears. I am getting why you no longer come for Christmas.

January 1

It has been a good day. Sally ran out of baking supplies and quit asking for more. Ronald's box of perilous prestidigitation seems to be vanishing piece by piece, each perhaps by its own charm. The magic wand snapped in half when he tried to pry apart some wire puzzles he had permanently joined, and while everyone denies stomping the silk hat, the imprint does match Sarah's sneaker. More power to her.

Happy New Year, Aunt Maggie.

P.S. I found my razor, CD, and other stuff this afternoon when I levitated Sally's oven up to the attic.

The Life and Times of Pixie Homaly Domaly

To give you the framework of people and time, it was in the summer of 1948 when we acquired the cocker spaniel in our grandparents' town of Loveland, Colorado. Jerry was going on eleven, Maureen had turned nine, I was pushing five, Jimmy was two, and Kathi was not yet a year old. Mickey Don and Timmy would join Pixie's family in 1949 and 1954.

I distinctly remember the drive back to Laramie. Jimmy and I were fighting over the red puppy on the floor of our station wagon. Our parents interceded with an offer to let Jimmy think of a name for her. In a burst of creativity he announced it, and she was on the spot christened by family proclamation Pixie Homaly Domaly.

Pixie was a family dog in the tradition of the middle of the last century. With sufficient urging, she might sit, shake, or roll, but that was about it. Unlike television's Lassie, the nation's dog of choice in our generation, Pixie was never challenged to rescue Timmy from a well.

She wore a collar with her tag dangling, but I doubt she was ever on a leash. She had the run of the neighborhood but mostly stayed close to our house on the Laramie River. She did venture out, though, and all too frequently, she came whimpering back to Mom with porcupine quills in her nose or smelling of skunk.

Pixie attracted a string of paramours to our corner of town, and her amorous activities could have served as a laboratory for the Knight kids to study birds and bees if our parents had seized the opportunity. If Dad spraying a garden hose full blast at Pixie and her suitor of the moment prompted our interest it was summarily dismissed. Such were the times we lived in.

Often on a beautiful summer's evening, some of us kids would take bedrolls to the backyard to sleep under the stars. I was particularly proud of the morning I awoke to find Pixie had delivered her latest litter of five at the foot of my blanket. I felt like she had delivered the gifts to me personally, and I graciously wanted to keep them all. Pixie bore dozens of very cute puppies over her lifetime, but Mom succeeded in moving every one of them to different families.

Dad kept a birdbath and feeders to attract songbirds, quite successfully, I might add. On the other hand, Pixie aspired not to bird watching but to bird catching. She never snared even one, but her leaping attempts betrayed Dad's avian hospitality, like an alligator at a five-star hotel. He was at once exasperated and bemused by her futile attempts. She kept on the chase until her final years when she became too heavy from her life's diet of table scraps.

It has been some sixty years, but I will always remember Pixie Homaly Domaly at the zenith of a skyward vault for a robin, her red cocker spaniel ears, as long as she was tall, spread like wings in flight.

Buckets and Buckets

*There's a hole in the bucket, dear Liza, dear Liza,
There's a hole in the bucket, dear Liza, a hole. Then fix
it, dear Henry, dear Henry, dear Henry. Then fix it, dear
Henry, dear Henry, fix it.*

Back in 1960 at Carnegie Hall, Harry Belafonte and the marvelous Odetta sung this old folk song in a duet. You can still hear that very performance today on the Internet.

Henry and Liza dramatized the importance of buckets in society. They are perfect vessels for carrying volumes of water, and before the advent of pumpers, firefighters formed brigades, passing water in a line, bucketful after bucketful.

The ancient Greeks and Romans used buckets for the bringing of wine, bucketful after bucketful. In later centuries, before beer was bottled, if one wanted a brew outside of the saloon, it was carried out, bucketful after bucketful, in galvanized containers called growlers. Gourds served nicely for those purposes as well, and the ancients even employed bladders taken from domesticated animals when they were finished using them.

For a bucket to be a bucket, in my humble opinion, it should have a wide, flat bottom to keep it upright. One may chisel one from a rock, I suppose, but the weight would make it inconvenient. Early people learned to shape and fire them from clay, but they were fragile. Durable leather buckets have been around for centuries. Coopers today still craft buckets from wood, useful for any liquid, but especially nice for churning ice cream. Metal buckets, lightweight and durable, have been the most popular since the Bronze Age.

Tom Sawyer used a bucket to get the fence painted, but he delegated the odious chore of applying the bucket's contents to another boy and somehow got himself paid in the process. I am not as clever as old Tom, but I have the same attitude as he did. A bucket is a very handy thing to keep paint in, but someone else can get it out. With a brush or a roller, it does not matter.

One who dies is said to have "kicked the bucket." A theory about the origin of that term holds that it comes from execution by hanging, where a noose would be tied around the neck of the executionee who would be standing on an overturned bucket. When the executioner kicked the bucket away, the executionee would become the executioned.

If there is a hole in your bucket, as Liza has expounded, then fix it, dear Henry, dear Henry, with a straw. If the straw is too long, cut it, dear Henry, with an axe. If the axe is too dull, sharpen it, dear Henry, on a stone. If the stone is too dry, wet it, dear Henry, with water that you may fetch with your bucket, dear Henry.

But there's a hole in my bucket, dear Liza, dear Liza, a hole. And that, dear reader, is the predicament of my entire essay.

A Mousekin Christmas

Robert E. Mouse would never admit to being a scholar, but he did read many books, and he knew a lot of cool stuff. He could explain black holes in space, the meanderings of marsupials, and the reason why his favorite movie should have been named Cretaceous Park, not Jurassic Park, because its dinosaurs were from that era, not the Jurassic age.

But Robert couldn't quite believe in Santa Claus. He wanted to, but how could one man go to about a hundred thousand million houses in one single night? When he asked his mom to explain this and the one about sliding down a chimney into a burning fire, she said, "Maybe you'd better ask your dad." All Pop could offer was, "There's more than one way to skin a cat." That wasn't even an answer, and it was gross. Even a cat, the sworn enemy of genus mouse, does not deserve that.

Most mice can sleep anywhere and anytime they want. But if curiosity can kill a cat, it keeps a mouse awake, and this Christmas Eve was curious indeed. While the rest of his family and the human pests in the house were sleeping, Robert E. Mouse skittered behind the sofa, up and over the big television, and in and around piles of envelopes and packages. He was poking through the nut dish when he heard a sudden oomph, grunt, shoop, and a resounding ta-da from the fireplace.

He peeked around a filbert, and there stood the jolly fellow, slapping at burning embers on his backside and dislodging clouds of soot. Merry eyes twinkled behind the fogged spectacles, and even as this magical human gasped for breath, he gave off a mighty energy. From his bag, he drew packages of all sizes and colors and found places for them in branches and under the tree. But a pretty package, except perhaps to gnaw on, is of no interest to your average mouse.

Then Santa dropped the emptied bag on the mantel and drew from his deep vest pocket a red pouch labeled "for the mice". He hopped about the room, depositing a handful of raisins behind the sofa, various seeds under the table, and cookie crumbs all around.

Treats were everywhere, and it was a most wonderful mousian feast.

For last, he saved Robert's favorite, a handful of candy-covered chocolate bits that he lined across the mantel to spell out, in strict alphabetical order, "m-m-m-m-m-m." Then Santa tossed the remaining tasty morsels into his own mouth, sucked in his great belly until he turned nearly blue, and, with a ho-ho-ho, an ooomph, a grunt, a shoop and ta-da, up the chimney he flew.

The skeptical mousekin had seen Santa Claus for himself and learned how he remembered all God's creatures at Christmas. From the mantel, Robert E. Mouse selected one shiny red m, skittered to his bed behind the refrigerator, made a pillow of his candy, and slept soundly through the rest of that magical night.

WHITE LIES AND PUFFERY

I was in the eighth grade, and Sister Mary Sarah led us through an interesting discussion of "little white lies." The boys especially seemed comfortable with the idea of fibs to avoid consequences, such as claiming to be doing homework to avoid taking out the trash or claiming to be finished with homework to get your dad to take you to Dairy Queen. Some of us could even justify a white lie that might make the world seem a better place, such as telling a boy dressed in rags that he looked nice. Sister acknowledged the ethical dilemma but reminded us that a lie even at its whitest is still a venial sin and would earn us time in purgatory.

In the battle of the sexes, white lies are strategy. "Your smile is lovely, your eyes are gorgeous, and your figure is exquisite." Or they are defense. "No, they don't make you look fat, dear." Or they are diversionary. "No, no, my darling, I didn't say broad in the beam."

I have carried Sister's Catholic school lesson into my seventies and still suffer a guilty pang when I offer a compliment that might not be completely heartfelt or an excuse that might not be completely honest. I will not likely be found out, but I know the price will be assessed in purgatory.

In the business world, white lies are called "puffery," and they are quite acceptable. For instance, I can place an ad claiming my cleaning service will give you the shiniest windows in the world, and I do not have to prove it. It is just puffery, and it is okay with the Federal Trade Commission.

In 2000, Pizza Hut sued Papa John's Pizza, claiming false advertising for using the slogan, "Better Ingredients, Better Pizza." Pizza Hut had just finished its own "Totally New Pizza" campaign, declaring war on poor quality pizza, touting the better taste of its own, and daring anyone to find any better. Papa John's lost to Pizza Hut in federal court, but the Fifth Circuit Court of Appeals in New Orleans reversed the decision with an analysis that concluded,

We think that non-actionable "puffery" comes in at least two possible forms: (1) an exaggerated, blustering, and boasting statement upon which no reasonable buyer would be justified in relying; or (2) a general claim of superiority over comparable products that is so vague that it can be understood as nothing more than a mere expression of opinion.

The decision was only one in a long string of similar court rulings, but it provided precedent to justify a big jewelry chain's claim of the finest in diamonds, a greasy spoon's claim to the most delicious pancakes, and everything that comes out of that ginsu guy's mouth.

As for those little white lies and me, I do not know if the Fifth Circuit has any sway in purgatory sentences, but I can hope.

Stars and Stripes and Sousa Forever

For as long as there are parades, the "Liberty Bell" and "Washington Post" marches will be staples of high school, college, and municipal bands throughout the world, but probably nothing in music ever evokes a greater response than "The Stars and Stripes Forever."

The morning after its introduction in May 1897, a Philadelphia reviewer declared the song "stirring enough to rouse the American eagle from its crag and set him to shriek exultantly." Another paper said, "The audience was not satisfied until they heard it three times ... The Sousa swing and vigor that have made all his compositions ... distinctive are very evident, and it will likely become as popular as its predecessors."

When its composer, the American master John Philip Sousa died in 1932, Will Rogers, yet another master, wrote,

> *He was in life rather small of stature. Not particularly impressive, very modest and unassuming. Yet he produced something that any hour of the day or night can quicken the blood and thrill the nerves of every American man, woman or child. His tunes were the Lincoln's Gettysburg address of music.*

When Arthur Fiedler directed the World Symphony Orchestra in 1972, he chose to end each concert with Sousa's famous march. He was criticized for presenting such a partisan piece on the world stage, but it brought standing ovations at every concert. Harold C. Shonberg, music critic for the *New York Times*, said in 1978, "'The Stars and Stripes Forever' may be the greatest piece of music ever written by an American composer." It became the national march of the United States by congressional act and the president's signature in 1987.

My son Thomas was part of a Colorado high school honors band that toured in Italy, Germany, Switzerland, and France. They played in public squares along the route, sometimes planned but often impromptu. Whenever they struck up "The Stars and Stripes Forever," it would inspire the crowd, regardless of the language or the country they were in, to stand and cheer from the opening stanza. Often the band would reprise the piece by acclimation.

John Philip Sousa was born in 1854. In 1880, he became the conductor of the United States Marine Band, and in 1892, he formed his own touring band. Every performance would see him in new white gloves and a uniform sporting some thirty-five yards of braid. Along the way, he invented the Sousaphone to deliver those rich, deep oom-pah-pahs felt in the collective seat of the pants of marching music enthusiasts all over the world.

Sousa said a march stimulates every center of vitality, awakens the imagination, and spurs patriotic impulses that may have been dormant for years. He insisted that all good marches must appeal to the musical and unmusical alike and he once declared that his music "could make a man with a wooden leg get up and march."

An Introduction to Chindogu

Have you ever noticed that a cat craving affection will rub up against your leg or the furniture until you finally give her the touch she is craving? Well, ladies and gentlemen, we now have the marvelous AutoPetter designed to exploit the energy of your pet's own perpetual motion. With it, kitty can pat her own head and scratch her own back, and she can then retire to her brand-new Zen Litter Box, a sanctuary for retreat and tranquility.

Those are examples of the art of Chindogu. You probably never have heard of it or the fact that there is an entire field of Chindogu inventors around the world. We visited this morning with one of the most prolific men in the discipline. Here are some excerpts from our conversation.

Q. What can you tell our readers, Percy Pamfrey, about the art of Chindogu?

Well, sir, Chindogu is a Japanese word that refers to an invention, any invention that is almost useless. For instance, there is the Hands-Free Walking Stick that you strap to your leg, or the Video Hat that will suspend your smartphone in front of you as you go through the day, allowing you to eat your lunch without ever putting down the device. I wish I could claim to be the inventor of either one of those babies.

Q. Would they make you rich?

No, they certainly would not, sir. The International Chindogu Society would never permit that. There are tenets that define the art and philosophy of Chindogu. While every Chindogu is an almost useless object, not every almost useless object is Chindogu.

In order to move from just almost useless to really almost useless, the creation must be useless for any practical purposes. If you invent something that you turn out to actually use, even just once, then you have failed at the art. Your idea must evolve to become a functioning prototype, but it may not be patented, and it must not be sold, even as a joke. And humor must not be the sole reason for creating a Chindogu. If it is funny, and it likely will be, it's simply the result of finding an elaborate solution to a problem that may not have been that pressing.

Q. All very interesting, Mr. Pamfrey. Can you give us more examples of Chindogu?

Well, is your refrigerator filling up with leftovers? Try a refrigerator Shelf Extender. Or how about wiper blades for your scuba mask?

I could go on, but first let me tell you about a current project of my own, the Pamfrey Perfecto Pea Parer.

Q. I had no idea that peas need paring, Mr. Pamfrey. Can you tell us how it would work?

Well now, that will be my secret, sir, but I can tell you, when my product hits the market, peas will be pared, and none will be spared. And for it all, I will win the Nobel Peas Prize.

But I'm not stopping there because, once I get Pea Parer out of the laboratory and into the market, I have yet another brainchild that will land me yet another Nobel, the one for literature. It's the Pamfrey Perfecto Paragraph Parer.

MAKING IT HOME

My good friend is a bright and interesting woman who spent too many childhood nights in the bomb shelters of war-torn Germany. Although I am still learning every day about her long life, I know she has experienced more than her share of tragedy. Today, she suffers from two separate eye diseases for which the treatments are severe and the testing is exhausting. I spoke to her briefly last week after a day of doctors' appointments, and she was glad just to be home.

Now, she faces the likelihood of soon losing her vision in one eye and the possibility in time of losing sight in the other. She speaks longingly about one more trip to Germany and the city that means home to her. I believe home to her also means that special place she makes in her heart for the memories of her beloved late husband, and when we reach the end of one of our regular Saturday shopping excursions, she often declares her happiness at just being home.

It is a complex topic, this whole idea of home. They say home is where the heart is, and you will get no argument from me. I look about my apartment, reflect on the touches I have brought to it, and feel gratified to be home. I feel at home when I drive down Grand Avenue in Laramie, the city of my birth. If I venture off to visit one of my sisters or brothers, I am home as soon as I am welcomed at the door.

I feel at home downtown in my office. Arriving there on a frigid January morning, I strategically bypass that section of the sidewalk at Eighteenth and Lawrence where a homeless man in a sleeping bag is sprawled on the cardboard bed he dragged to the warmth of a steam vent. How can the idea of home mean anything to him? Does it even exist in his world? Is home the slab he is sleeping on? Is home a place or even places far away lost in the memories of long ago? Or is home to him the emotional shelter of that bottle jealously guarded under his coat?

Red Skelton entertained us in the fifties with many characters, but my favorite was Freddy the Freeloader, the hobo who made his home in the city dump. He furnished his corrugated castle with decrepit pieces dragged in from the junk piles that made up his estate. He gave it the love and pride of a tidy homeowner, including an elaborate feather dusting of the rickety old table and an exaggerated sweeping of the dirt floor. He would finish his chores by adjusting an old sampler hanging from a tack on his cardboard wall and, with a flourish, stand back to soak in its simple message, "Home Sweet Home."

Freddie the hobo would never be homeless, and nor, for the grace of God, will I.

Live to Learn

Permit me to be a bit introspective. I learned a new word today, and by definition, it describes me. It turns out I am an autodidact, meaning somebody whose knowledge is self-taught. How well I'm doing at it is for others to judge, but knowing I am one makes me feel right with the world, and the fact I learned the word in the process of being the word is especially satisfying.

It strikes me that, no matter the level of formal education one achieves, a fulfilled person is one who is a lifelong learner. A doctor of philosophy at the age of seventy may find the same fascination in learning about lizards as her grandson would at the age of seven. The opportunity to be an autodidact is there for both of them, as it is for every person on the earth.

Science-fiction novelist Robert Heinlein, in *Time Enough for Love*, defined the essence of a lifelong learner.

> *A human being should be able to change a diaper, plan an invasion, butcher a hog, conn a ship, design a building, write a sonnet, balance accounts, build a wall, set a bone, comfort the dying, take orders, give orders, cooperate, act alone, solve equations, analyze a new problem, pitch manure, program a computer, cook a tasty meal, fight efficiently, die gallantly. Specialization is for insects.*

I have the highest admiration for those who are formally educated in the sciences as well as the arts and respect the work and sacrifices they have made to get there. I am not sure what it is in my own character that admires degrees when accomplished by others but eschews the process for myself. Maybe it is a matter of impatience, lack of confidence, or a combination of both.

While my own résumé does not reflect college credentials, I can hope it demonstrates a degree of learning by dint of professional and personal accomplishment. At every stage of my life, I have competed, collaborated, and held my own with well-educated people. What could be more rewarding than that?

There is some irony in knowing it has taken me seventy years to discover the word "autodidact" and yet how it so closely defines me. I call myself semiretired these days, but I do so not to take it easier but for time to take more in, knowing that every morning brings another day of learning.

I am sorry to leave you now, but I have some didacting to do.

CPSIA information can be obtained at www.ICGtesting.com
Printed in the USA
LVOW05s0922250714

395885LV00001B/1/P